ISBN 978-1-333-79319-7
PIBN 10632686

1 MONTH OF
FREE
READING

at

www.ForgottenBooks.com

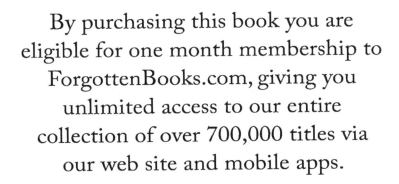

By purchasing this book you are eligible for one month membership to ForgottenBooks.com, giving you unlimited access to our entire collection of over 700,000 titles via our web site and mobile apps.

To claim your free month visit:
www.forgottenbooks.com/free632686

THE TECHNIQUE and ART

OF

ORGAN PLAYING

BY

CLARENCE DICKINSON

M. A., LITT. D., MUS. DOC.

With the collaboration of
H. A. DICKINSON
M. A., PH. D.

Fifth Printing

Paper Cover $3.50
Boards $4.00 Cloth $5.00

NEW YORK ∴ THE H. W. GRAY CO.
SOLE AGENTS FOR NOVELLO & CO., Ltd.

CONTENTS

PART I. TEXT

6

PART II. MUSIC

MUSICAL COMPOSITIONS INCLUDED IN PART II

PREFACE

————

This book is designed to provide the teacher with the technical material necessary to carry the student from the beginning of his studies through to the acquirement of complete command of his instrument. The aim has been to include in one volume a study of all the distinctive principles of organ technique, with enough illustrations and exercises through which they may be mastered, together with interesting compositions which will at once call for their application.

It is hoped that the textual division, Part I, may prove of value in saving the teacher's time by supplying a book of reference for students and also by providing material from which themes may be drawn for class conferences in which these points may be discussed and enlarged upon.

In assembling in one volume studies of all the various points of organ technique necessary to the equipment of the organist with as detailed a description as possible of the process by which each is to be mastered, the author has had in mind, also, the many students who must pursue their work without the personal guidance of a teacher. To the studio of every teacher there come pupils who are able to remain only a short time, who then, although eager for further study, are obliged to return to their posts to do the best they can for their further advancement in their art, and to teach others out of their still limited equipment. Of course nothing can ever take the place of the personal guidance and example of an inspired teacher; this book simply aims to provide the "next best thing" for students who must continue their studies thus or not at all. With their needs in view the author has endeavored, in Part I, to take up each point of technique in logical and related order, and to describe it clearly and definitely, with illustrations whenever they may aid in comprehension and application; and, in Part II, to supply, also in logical order, just as many exercises as are absolutely necessary to cover each point, and pieces which, although they demand the application of each point of technique as it is acquired and are therefore excellent studies, are never mere studies, but are such as will be of use to the organist always, and of so great variety in style that effective recital programs can be made from just these numbers.

PART I

CHAPTER I

THE ORGAN AS AN INSTRUMENT

AS one of the most ancient instruments of music the organ had its origin in the flute, a wind or "flue" instrument which readily suggested itself to primitive man when he found he could make a musical sound by blowing through a stalk of bamboo or other reed. In the development of the organ this "flue" has been multiplied into many pipes which are set on a chest and controlled by keys which let into them the wind furnished by centrifugal fans which may be operated by man-power, by water, or by electricity.

The ancient flute had holes along the side by which the player could obtain variety of pitch. The shorter the pipe the higher the pitch of tone it gives forth, and the flute player could shorten or lengthen his pipe at will by putting his finger on one of these holes. In the organ, instead of boring holes along the side of one pipe, a set of pipes of different lengths is constructed in each tone quality; these are known as "ranks" of pipes. They may vary in length from an inch and a half to sixty-four feet, and in circumference from the small metal pipes the size of a lead pencil to wooden pipes so large that a Shetland pony can stand inside.

Certain ranks of pipes are controlled from the keyboards for the hands, known as manuals; others, less extensive, from the keyboard for the feet, known as the pedal.

An organ which has only one manual always consists of what is known as the Great organ. This is the descendant of the ancient Roman Hydraulus, or water organ, invented by Ctesibius of Alexandria in the third century B.C., of which a model was found when the ruins of Carthage were excavated, and which was probably modeled on a much older instrument, such as the one of ten keys with ten pipes to each key, of tremendously powerful tone, which is described in the Talmud as part of the furnishing of the Temple at Jerusalem.

If there are two manuals the lower will be the Great and the upper the Swell organ. The volume of tone of the ancient Great organ was, of necessity, always full and unvaried. In 1711 Abraham Jordan and his son, of London, conceived the idea of enclosing an organ in a chest with shuttered sides which could be opened and closed gradually by means of ropes attached to a pedal, thus enabling the organist to swell and diminish the tone at will. This "Swelling" organ was then incorporated in the same case with the Great organ and provided with its own keyboard. It is still known as the Swell organ and the pedal by which it is operated as the Swell pedal.

In some modern organs the idea of the Swell has been extended to apply to the other organs also, so that each organ — the Great and the Choir as well as the Swell — is enclosed in its own separate swell box, thus giving the player control over the dynamic resources of his entire instrument.

The ancient Great organ in the cathedrals and churches, in which, as we have seen, any means of controlling the tremendous volume of sound was lacking, could not be used to accompany the singing of the choir. A smaller instrument was used for this purpose, which was at first portable, but which, when it was gradually enlarged until it became too big to carry about, was given a fixed position and was therefore known as a Positive. This is the present Choir organ. In order to make it possible for one organist to play both solo and accompanying instruments this Positive was moved up behind his bench, so that he could play his organ numbers on the Great organ, then swing around on the bench and accompany the choir on the Positive. At last it occurred to some one as yet anonymous to set this Choir organ in the case with the Great, giving it its own keyboard, as had been done with the Swell organ. In this transference its manual was given a different place in different countries; the arrangement in America, as in England, when an organ has three manuals is as follows:

Upper — Swell
Middle — Great
Lower — Choir

7

8

If there is a fourth manual it is known as the Solo organ and is placed above the other manuals; in it are assembled special solo stops and stops of extra heavy pressure.

A fifth manual is rarely found on the most modern organs in this country, but when there is one it is usually devoted to what is known as the Echo or Celestial organ. In the sixteenth century an organist in the Netherlands conceived the idea of enclosing some of the pipes of the organ in a box to gain softness and an illusion of distance. This enclosed organ produces the effect suggested by its name. Now, however, the Echo organ is seldom given a manual of its own, but can be played from one or two of the other manuals.

The Pedal organ was, in the beginning, and as late as the closing years of the fifteenth century, nothing more than a clamp which held down a bass note or two. In 1470 Master Bernhard, organist of St. Mark's, Venice, put a pedal keyboard in the floor and attached it with ropes to draw down the bass keys of the manuals. In the seventeenth century the pedal keyboard, greatly enlarged, was given independent inner works, and the Pedal organ created.

We have already referred to the great number of pipes in the organ and to the fact that difference in pitch is obtained by making a difference in the length of pipes which produce the same tone quality. If we draw the stop on the Great organ marked 8-foot we get the pitch which corresponds to that of the piano. It receives its name because the organ keyboard begins at CC and the pipe which sounds that tone is eight feet long. The pipes controlled by the stop marked 4-foot are four feet in length and sound an octave higher than the 8-foot. Those marked 2-foot sound two octaves higher; added to the 8-foot stops these brighten the tone. A 16-foot stop — sometimes spoken of as a "double" — sounds an octave lower than an 8-foot; a 32-foot, two octaves lower. Used on the manuals these possess a somber, thick quality; they should be employed sparingly, therefore, and with discrimination. The 8-foot tone is the normal pitch and must form the foundation of all regular organ work.

On the ancient Great organ there was no means of regulating the volume of sound. When a key was pressed all the pipes of that pitch sounded at once, so that the noise was overpowering. In the sixteenth century an organist in the Netherlands devised a plan for shutting off the sound of any rank of pipes as desired, by means of slides manipulated by levers which stopped the wind from entering the pipes. These levers were known as stops, and the stops of the organ still perform their original function; when pushed in each one stops the wind from entering its own set of pipes; when drawn the obstruction is removed and the pipes are free to speak in response to the pressing of the keys. By a sort of figure of speech the name "stop" has come to be applied not only to the lever but to the ranks of pipes which it controls; thus we speak of Flute stops, Diapason stops, when we mean ranks of Flute pipes, ranks of Diapason pipes, and so on.

When there are a great many stops on an organ the organist is now enabled to draw whole groups at one time by means of "pistons" placed between keyboards, or by "toe pistons" or combination pedals placed above the pedal keyboard, each of which will control a definite group of stops. Two manuals may be made to speak at the same time, or the pedal organ and any manual, by drawing "couplers," which are tilting tablets, usually placed above the upper manual, which couple, for instance, Swell to Great, Swell to Pedal, Swell to Swell-Super-Octave, and so forth.

By means of a remarkable device known as the "Crescendo Pedal" the organist can draw all the stops in the organ in dynamic succession, building up to full organ and reducing the tone again to silence. Speaking generally, full organ tone is built as follows: Draw first the softest 8-foot stop, gradually add the 8-foot stops and 4-foot stops one by one in order of power; then the 16-foot; then the 2-foot; then the heavy Reeds and Mixtures. Of course this is the barest outline of procedure, which must be varied to suit each individual instrument. A smooth *crescendo* is the desideratum; the stop added next in each case must be the one which makes the least appreciable difference in the volume of tone.*

CLASSIFICATION OF STOPS

With respect to quality of tone and the manner of its production, stops, that is to say ranks of pipes, are divided into two main classes: Flues, or Labials, in which the sound is produced by setting in vibration the column of air inside the pipes, and Reeds, or Linguals, in which the sound is produced by the vibrating of a tongue, or "reed," within the pipes.

---

* For a more detailed history of the organ as an instrument see Dickinson's "Excursions in Musical History."

Flues are subdivided into four classes: I. Diapasons; II. (a) Flutes, (b) Gedackt; III. Strings, also spoken of as Gamba tone; IV. the Gemshorn, a hybrid family. On an instrument of good size the stops in each of these classes would be disposed about as follows:*

I. DIAPASONS; ALSO CALLED PRINCIPALS

GREAT	16' Diapason	CHOIR	16' Diapason
	8' Diapason		8' Diapason, Geigen Principal
	4' Octave		8' Dulciana
	2⅔' Twelfth		4' Octave
	2' Fifteenth		Mixtures seldom
	Some Mixtures		
		SOLO	8' Stentorphone
SWELL	16' Dulciana		
	16' Diapason	PEDAL	32' Diapason
	8' Diapason		16' Diapason
	8' Vox Angelica		8' Octave
	4' Octave		4' Octave
	2' Flautino		
	Some Mixtures		

II. FLUTES AND GEDACKT

GREAT	16' Bourdon	CHOIR	16' Bourdon
	8' Clarabella		8' Gedackt
	8' Harmonic Flute		8' Melodia
	8' Gross Flute		8' Concert Flute
	8' Doppel Flute		8' Flute Celeste
	4' Flute		8' Quintadena
			4' Flute d'Amour
			4' Suabe Flute
SWELL	16' Bourdon, or Lieblich Gedackt		2⅔' Nazard
	8' Rohr Flute, Gedackt		2' Piccolo
	8' Chimney Flute	SOLO	8' Harmonic Flute
	8' Flute Celeste		8' Concert Flute
	8' Clarabella		4' Suabe Flute
	8' Spitz Flute		4' Harmonic Flute
	8' Stopped Diapason or Gedackt	PEDAL	32' Bourdon
	4' Harmonic Flute		16' Bourdon
	2' Piccolo		16' Lieblich Gedackt
			8' Flute
			8' Still Gedackt
			4' Flute

"Mixtures" are so called because they sound, not a single tone but a chord. For instance: when low C is played with a Mixture stop drawn, instead of hearing CC you hear the chord e, g, c. Moreover, the pitch is slightly different, because the Mixture intervals are not tempered, for the reason that they are used to reinforce the overtones, and overtones are natural. Tempering is man's invention; nature's overtones are not tempered.

A "Harmonic" stop is created by taking a pipe of double the length necessary and piercing a hole about the middle of its length, or at a point which will give the desired pitch. The extra length of pipe gives additional fullness, richness, and, at the same time, brilliancy of tone.

The Dulciana and the Vox Angelica are really very soft Diapasons, but as they are so soft that they take on a String tone they are used as Strings and are usually classified as such, except purely technically.

* A detailed study of the subject of organ stops is found in "Organ Stops and Their Artistic Registration," by George Ashdown Audsley.

III. STRINGS, OR GAMBA TONE

GREAT	8' Gamba	CHOIR	16' Contra-Gamba
	8' Viole d'Amour		16' Dulciana
	8' Keraulophone		8' Dulciana
			8' Dulcet
SWELL	16' Contra-Gamba		8' Unda Maris
	8' Viole d'Orchestre		8' Dulciana
	8' Unda Maris		4' Viola
	8' Viole d'Amour	SOLO	8' Gamba
	8' Salicional		8' Gamba Celeste
	8' Voix Celeste	PEDAL	16' Violone
	8' Aeoline		16' Gamba
	4' Violina		16' Dulciana
	4' Celestina		8' Violoncello
			8' Gamba

There is a hybrid family of stops, the Gemshorn family, of which the tone is a combination of soft String tone and Flute tone, in color more nearly a String or soft Diapason tone. It includes

8' Gemshorn	8' Erzähler	Some Mixtures
4' Gemshorn	8' Kleine Erzähler	

Reeds may be roughly divided into two classes:

I. Chorus Reeds, which correspond to the brass of the orchestra.

II. Orchestral Reeds, which correspond to the woodwinds of the orchestra.

I. CHORUS REEDS: BRASS, TRUMPET TONE

GREAT	16' Ophicleide	SOLO	16' Ophicleide
	16' Tuba		8' Tuba
	8' Trumpet		8' Tuba Mirabilis
	4' Clarion		4' Clarion
SWELL	16' Posaune or Horn		
	8' Trumpet	PEDAL	32' Bombarde
	8' Cornopean		16' Ophicleide
	8' Oboe		16' Posaune or Trombone
	4' Clarion		8' Trumpet
CHOIR	16' Horn or		8' Tuba
	8' Horn		4' Clarion
	8' Trumpet or Tuba		

II. ORCHESTRAL REEDS: WOODWIND TONE

GREAT	16' Horn	SOLO	8' Orchestral Oboe
SWELL	8' Cornopean		8' English Horn
	8' Oboe		8' French Horn
	8' Flügelhorn		8' Clarinet (or Corno di
	8' Vox Humana		Bassetto)
CHOIR	16' Fagotto (Bassoon)		8' Heckelphone
	8' Clarinet		8' Musette
	8' Flügelhorn	PEDAL	16' Horn
	8' Orchestral Oboe		16' Fagotto
	8' English Horn		
	8' French Horn		

CHAPTER II

MANUAL TOUCHES

The acquirement of keyboard technique at the piano is essential in preparation for the study of organ, as there is so much else to attend to on the latter instrument from the very beginning of study that the student cannot afford to devote time to gaining finger flexibility and agility.

POSITION AT THE ORGAN

The first point of attention for the organ student is the very important one of his position at the instrument. It is necessary for the organist to seat himself exactly in the middle of the organ bench and to stay there without sliding around. To admit of this and of the proper manual and pedal technique the bench must be the right height, which is twenty inches from the top of middle D on the pedal keyboard to the top of the organ seat. It is an exceedingly common practice of builders to make the bench about two inches too high, on the theory that it is easier to cut it down than to build it up; but the almost invariable outcome is that the seat always remains as it was built. The high bench is responsible for much poor organ playing, as the player is obliged to sit on the edge of the seat instead of being able to maintain the perfect balance possible only when he is seated squarely and solidly in the middle, and which is essential to physical, and therefore to technical control. The organ student should never proceed to even his first hour of practice without making sure that the bench is exactly the right height.

Sit down on the organ bench so that, with the feet close together, touching, the left foot will fall on C and the right on D. Hold yourself perfectly erect; do not loll; keep the elbows close to the body; do not bend over when you reach for a stop, but use your arm and not your whole body. When you reach for a pedal note swing your legs as on a pivot and keep the torso facing the keyboard. Insist to yourself upon holding this proper and erect position and playing "quietly," that is to say without unnecessary, ungraceful, and distracting motions. If you insist on it at first it will soon become second nature and you will never feel the slightest inclination towards anything more lax. In his description of Bach's playing, Forkel, after telling how the great master used his hands and feet, adds, "The other parts of his body took no part in the performance."

When you have assumed the correct position, and ascertained exactly the proper distance at which you as an individual should be removed from the keyboard when playing, it is highly advisable to fasten a block of wood on the floor to hold your organ bench at that distance, so that it can never vary.

ATTACK AND RELEASE OF KEYS

Organ touch differs from piano touch as greatly as the keys of the two instruments differ in action. A key of the piano is a lever which sets in motion a hammer with which a string is struck; a key of the organ simply completes an electric circuit, and such resistance as is offered is the artificial resistance of a spring put in to create it. The keys of the piano must, therefore, always be struck; the keys of the organ are *pressed* in legato playing, and struck only when brilliant staccato effects are desired, and even then always with a much less degree of force than is employed in piano playing.*

The very first technical point to which the student should direct his attention is that of attack and release of a key; the matter of release is much more important on the organ than on the piano, since the organ tone is sustained with full power as long as the key is held, whereas the piano tone dies away in any case. It is essential, then, first of all, to practise the attack and release of single notes, then of thirds and chords, in definite rhythm.

---

* The subject of Organ Touch is here treated with reference to organs with electric or pneumatic action; the old mechanical action is passing so rapidly that it does not now require detailed consideration.

11

LEGATO TOUCH

The characteristic touch of the organ is the legato touch and its acquirement is the first and absolute essential of organ playing. The Italian principle of *bel canto*, "He who cannot join his notes cannot sing," applies with emphasis to those who would play the organ. This legato touch is a most delicate matter and demands the cultivation of great sensitiveness of touch and hearing. It is acquired in the first place by keeping the fingers always touching the keys, not raising them at all. This is entirely possible on an instrument the keys of which are pressed, not struck.

With relation to the instrument this is the principle of legato touch: when you press down a key, at a point about an eighth of an inch down a spring offers some resistance to the player, and at that moment the pipe begins to speak. In letting go the key again it is at the moment at which this spring is released that the sound ceases. If you play on two keys in succession there will be a moment at which your first key ceases to sound and a moment at which the second key begins to sound. Legato playing means that these shall be not two different moments but one and the same moment; a fraction of miscalculation in letting the second key come on too soon means that the notes blur; if it does not come on soon enough the tones are separated and the playing is not legato. Great delicacy of digital and aural perception and the perfect correlation of the two are, therefore, essential, as well as the acquirement of finished technique. Because of its high demands this most distinctive feature of really good organ playing is most rare, and it is worth while to bend one's best endeavors towards its mastery.

SUBSTITUTION

There are many passages in which with the ordinary fingering you would use on the piano it would be impossible to maintain a true organ legato. In many of these cases the problem can be solved by the employment of "Substitution," which is effected in two ways: I. Finger Substitution, II. Hand Substitution.

I. Substitution of one finger for another on a key is frequently necessary in playing successive chords, as, for example, in the following passages in thirds and sixths:

II. Substitution of one hand for another is employed when, for instance, the organist begins to play on a different manual, draws a stop, turns a page of music, or employs one hand to direct the choir.

THUMB GLISSANDO

But perfect legato playing demands even more than the skillful management of the fingers usually employed in playing an instrument. To acquire it you must treat each hand as if it were equipped with six fingers instead of only five. The second joint of the thumb, or, to be more exact, the side of the thumb between the first and second joints, is to be considered an extra finger; and the side of the thumb between the second joint and the third, or axis, is also to be treated as an independent finger. The employment of these two extras is known as "Thumb Glissando." The pianistic significance of the term *glissando* is applied in organ playing also for white note passages which, because too rapid to be played by the fingers in the ordinary way, are executed by drawing the finger nail swiftly over the keys. In itself, however, the term signifies "with gliding motion," and this is its significance when applied to thumb technique in organ playing, when it is designated as "Thumb Glissando"; it is an indispensable aid to perfect legato playing. Thumb Glissando I implies sliding from one key to another on the cushion of the tip of the thumb; Thumb Glissando II implies playing on the part of the thumb between the first and second joints; Thumb Glissando III implies playing on the part of the thumb between the second joint and axis — these two latter, of course, always in connection with the use of the tip of the thumb, which plays the next succeeding note.

Thumb Glissando I. In passing from a black key to a white, or, rarely, from black to black or white to white, simply slide from one key to the other with gliding motion. This form of glissando may be employed by the fingers also.

Thumb Glissando II. When you are playing sixths with thirds on the white keys only, scale of C, as for instance

you have only two fingers, 4 and 2, with which to play the three new notes; the thumb has to slide over to D. Use the first joint of the thumb as an extra finger to hold down the E as you shove the thumb over so that the tip depresses D as the two upper fingers depress the next notes, B and F. The hand will be raised a trifle to effect this. The legato will not be interrupted in the slightest degree, as it would be by any other method of approach to D.

In a descending scale passage the thumb moves along thus, performing double duty as if it were two thumbs, and the effect is that of "picking off" smoothly note after note, maintaining a perfect legato. Illustrations of this will be found in Part II, Section V.

In an ascending scale passage, as:

with the fingers well in on the keys the hand is raised from the wrist until the thumb is almost upright on E; the hand is pulled out and down over the keyboard so that the tip of the thumb slides smoothly to F as the other two fingers move to A and D. The wrist is raised again and the operation repeated.

Thumb Glissando III. When playing sixths and thirds involving black keys, that is to say in any other scale than C, it is necessary to employ the second joint of the thumb, or, more strictly speaking, to play on the side of the cushion of the thumb between the second joint and the axis. For example, if you are moving from

in order to move from F to E♭ without breaking the legato you must shove the thumb in as far as possible on the keyboard, just as far as G and E will permit you, that is, until the cushion of the thumb strikes against the edge of the G key. Thus, holding down the F with the second joint of the thumb (or the part between the second and third joints), you will find that the tip of the thumb will reach over to E♭ and you can connect the two notes without the slightest break in the legato.

You will note the necessity for the employment of all three forms of glissando in, for example, the scale of D♭ in which

Gliss. III   Gliss. II   Gliss. I   III   II   II   I

you employ: firstly, Glissando III: Hold F with the cushion between the second joint and the axis of the thumb and depress E♭ with the tip of the thumb; secondly, Glissando II: Pass from E♭ to D♭ "picking off" smoothly with the first joint of the thumb; thirdly, Glissando I: Pass from D♭ to C with simple glissando. The tip of the thumb is now on C; to pass to B♭ it is necessary to shove the hand in as far as it will go; to reach the position of playing on the side of the thumb between the second joint and the axis (Glissando III again). The other movements demanded by this scale are repetitions of these, as indicated.

Going up this scale, you cannot pass up Glissando I from a white to a black note, so you will be obliged to play on the first-to-second or second-to-third joints, as the skip may demand — Glissando II or III — and the tip of the thumb, when you pass from a white note to a black. Thus, E♭ to F will call for Glissando III; F to G♭ for Glissando II.

CROSSING A LONGER FINGER OVER A SHORTER

Yet another aid in maintaining a perfect legato is the employment of a practice in fingering which is peculiar to the organ: passing a longer finger over a shorter. Thus, when the fifth finger is occupied, the third or fourth may be passed over the top of it to depress the next key above without the interruption of the legato which would be occasioned by any other procedure.

IMPORTANCE OF A PERFECT LEGATO

Any one who has ever watched Alexandre Guilmant, the master who attained the most perfect legato we have known in organ playing, could not fail to be struck by the manner in which his hands seemed to creep over the keys, as it were, weaving in and out. The foregoing principles were the secret of that wonderful legato, which he maintained with unremitting care. Other players there were who were at times his equal in this regard and who might be even more brilliant in inspired moments, sweeping the listener along with them with irresistible power, yet, when they were indisposed and "didn't feel like it" their technique suffered a lapse and their playing was of comparatively little interest; but so unfailingly had Guilmant observed all these points of technique, never permitting himself an instant's carelessness, that they had become second nature to him, so that even when he was indisposed or uninspired — as every human artist must be at times — he never failed to maintain interest by the revelation of perfect technique, and, in numbers in which it was demanded, that exquisite legato which was the admiration of all.

It may sound rather singular to say that true legato playing is even more important on a small organ than on a large one, but, as a matter of fact, the fewer the resources of the organ the more imperative is perfection in the elemental matter of quality of touch. A large instrument offers so many effects of volume and color that it may be possible to make quite an impression without doing any really very good playing, but on a very small one each note stands forth naked and bare, and the effect can too easily be one of naught but a "kist o' whistles." Only the employment of a true legato touch can so bind the tones together as to produce solidity and make a degree of contrast possible.

TOUCHES OTHER THAN LEGATO

Nevertheless, though a fine legato is the *sine qua non* of good organ playing, the organist must beware of using it exclusively; unvaried legato playing is deadly. Its beauty can be fully brought out only by being thrown into relief by the employment of other touches when they are suitable. These others give life and vigor, forcefulness and brilliancy to organ playing and must be carefully acquired. The four main touches employed in organ playing are

I. Legato, indicated (if at all) by a slur, thus:

II. Semi-detached, Non-Legato, upon occasion Brillante, indicated by slur and dots, thus: ․ ․ ․ ․

III. Marcato, indicated by line or dot and line, thus:

IV. Staccato, indicated by dot, thus: ⸱ꝑ

II. The semi-detached, non-legato, or brillante touch implies the slightest possible separation between the notes. It is used in passages which are legato in effect, but which if played absolutely legato sound blurred, especially if a heavy body of tone is demanded, or low-pitched stops are used, or the building has a marked echo. The touch is acquired by curving the fingers so as to play with the very tips. In rapid legato passages that must be played at a tempo which makes blurring probable, or when the keys are moist and sticky or slippery, as in hot weather, a brillante touch which gives an effect of very clean yet flowing playing is obtained by curving the fingers so as to play on the tips of the nails. So, for instance, in the Bach D major Fugue, in which there must be not the slightest overhang or blur:

This was the touch employed by the late Dr. Heinrich Reimann, the greatest German Bach player, who, after years of Bach study and research, used to affirm unhesitatingly that this was Bach's own method of obtaining crystal-clear yet smooth effects in rapid playing.

III. Marcato touch stresses the note by giving it — according as it is a long or a short note — only from seven-eighths to three-quarters its nominal or face value, so as to create a separation between it and the note following. An effect of accent is thus produced, for which reason the marcato touch is much used in organ playing (see also the chapter on "Accent"). In very rapid passages it is practically impossible to differentiate the marcato and brillante touches; in passages in slow tempo marcato touch will give the note seven-eighths of its value while brillante will give it about fifteen-sixteenths.

GUILMANT, Sonata III

By the employment of marcato touch attention may be called to a melody, or it may be given added impressiveness and forcefulness. This will be appreciated if some such experiment is tried as the following: play these opening measures of the "Pilgrims' Chorus" legato:

The melody is pleasing, rather sentimental; play them marcato: it is instinct with pulsing life, vigor, and virile forcefulness.

IV. Staccato touch separates each note sharply from its fellows. This touch is acquired not by lifting the fingers as on the piano, but by shaking the wrist; the action which in piano playing is proper to the fingers is transferred to the wrist, the finger which is about to strike a note being merely depressed a trifle below the level of the other fingers. Studies in touches other than legato will be found in Part II, Sections X, XI.

CHAPTER III

PEDAL TECHNIQUE

The pedal keyboard on modern organs runs from CC to g; on older organs it extends only to f, and on older still only to d. On mediæval organs still in use in Europe it extends from D to d only.

Since pedal work demands a clean and sensitive pedal touch the organist should wear shoes which are as narrow as is consistent with perfect comfort, and made on a straight last so that the soles do not project. They should be of medium weight; too heavy shoes are unwieldy and interfere with the sensitiveness of the foot, while soles that are too thin are apt to overtire the more delicate foot muscles.

Before beginning practice it is well to glance at your organ pedals to make sure that they are clean, smooth, and slippery. You can no more do good work with muddy, sticky pedals than you could with molasses on your piano keys. Upon one occasion when Guilmant was playing at the Schola Cantorum, Paris, he seated himself on the organ bench, looked down at the pedals, got up and went out. The audience wondered greatly. In a few moments a man came in with a cloth and cleaned and polished the pedal keys, whereupon the great organist resumed his seat and began the recital.

When you have seated yourself in the middle of your organ bench put your feet down straight and close together, the left on C, the right on D. The feet should be flat on the keys. Some older instruction books direct the student to play with the tips of the toes; you have only to look at the shoes in the illustrations accompanying the directions in those books to see that this was the method of half a century ago, for which the too high organ bench was largely responsible. The foot should be flat on the key, the playing done on the ball of the foot.

The ankle movement corresponds to the wrist movement in manual technique, and most students will find their ankles amazingly stiff, as in ordinary life they do not seem to be used in such a manner as to make them as flexible as wrists usually are, and their flexibility has not been increased to the same extent by piano practice.

The relation of manual and pedal positions may be clearer if you will sit down in the position for playing, with the elbows close to the body, and take time to note how the arms from the elbows parallel the legs from the hips, and how the feet move from the ankles as the hands from the wrists. A certain amount of side-to-side movement is possible for the ankle without moving the leg, as it is for the wrist without moving the forearm; limbering up the ankles means simply acquiring that side-to-side movement.

The acquirement of correct and beautiful touch — and of the various touches — is as important for the pedals as for the manuals. In legato playing the student should strive to approach the degree of perfection demanded in finger legato. The principle is the same: the keys are *pressed*, not struck. When you play upon two keys in succession there will be one moment at which your first key ceases to sound, and a moment at which the second key begins to sound; legato playing means that these shall not be two different moments, but one and the same moment. Legato playing on the pedals is more difficult, for a beginner at least, than on the manuals.

POSITIONS FOR PLAYING INTERVALS WITHIN AN OCTAVE

Do not look at the pedals during your pedal practice; be on your guard from the beginning against forming this habit. Put your knees together and acquire the following positions for the intervals, playing them legato — you only press the keys, you do not strike them. Be sure to keep your knees together. One well-known organist in Paris was obliged, as a student, to strap his knees together for a time when practising in order to fix the habit.

To play a Second:

Bring the feet together, touching. For example, when the left foot is on C and you want to make the right foot play D, bring it up until it clicks (noiselessly) against the left foot.

To play a Third:

Bring the feet together so that the ankles touch. Do not forget that your knees must *always* be held together.

To play a Fourth:

The heels touch and the ankle bones touch, with the toes turned out as far as possible.

To play a Fifth:

The knees must touch, and the heels, with the toes turned out as far as possible without strain.

To play an Octave:

The knees must be together and the feet turned out, separated, to what seems to be their greatest stretch at a natural angle without any straining.

The Fourth, Fifth, and Octave — the Subdominant, Dominant, Tonic — are the most important positions, as of the most frequent occurrence.

The remaining intervals are found from those already acquired.

To play a Sixth:

Take the position for a Fifth and play the next note above.

To play a Seventh:

Assume the position for the Octave and play the next note below. These two intervals are always the hardest to play, just as they are the most difficult in sight-singing, in which they are found in exactly the same way.

This takes care of everything up to the Octave; it is easy to find one over the Octave, in the same manner as one below. A step greater than this is rare in simpler music, in hymns, simple anthems, and vocal accompanying, and by the time the student reaches the more elaborate he will be sufficiently at home on all parts of the keyboard to put his foot anywhere, at will.

Sufficient practice with this system will fix the intervals so that you will not need to look at the pedal keyboard any more than you do at the manuals. Nor will you need to fall back upon other aids sometimes suggested, such as always verifying your notes by first touching the nearest black note. Do not allow yourself to yield to this weakness, indulgence in it destroys your confidence. One who has taught many organists realizes how many are veritable slaves to this "black note habit."

LEGATO TOUCH ON THE PEDALS

Legato touch on the pedals is obtained in four ways:
I. With alternate feet; II. With toe and heel; III. Glissando; IV. Substitution.

In scale playing we start with the general principle that the first five notes of the scale are played with the left foot, the other three with the right foot. Naturally, this principle is modified as more and more black notes enter. To play the scale of C, for example: beginning with the left foot, when the toe depresses C raise the heel just enough to move it over on top of D; then depress the heel, raising the toe barely enough to slide over D to the top of E. Do not raise toe or heel any higher than is absolutely necessary; remember that you do not strike the note, but press it with the side of the sole, the ball of the foot, with the same character of touch as that employed in legato playing on the manuals.

Do not forget that when the right foot comes up to take its first note it must click (noiselessly) against the left in order to make sure of striking the correct note cleanly; it will blur if the right foot is not tight against the left.

Λ above the note signifies right toe, Λ below the note signifies left toe.
U above the note signifies right heel, U below the note signifies left heel.

In other scales, when you are about to pass from a white key to a black key the heel on the white key must be just near enough the black key to permit of depressing the black key with the toe. When playing on white and black keys alternately play a little farther in on the keyboard than when playing on white keys only.

When a foot has finished playing a note, leave it lightly where it is, conveniently at hand for its next note. Do not put it away back under the bench so that it will take a long time to bring it in from a distance when you need it again.

In the D major scale we find the first exception to the general rule of pedaling, as a black key occurs in the first five notes, namely F♯ this is taken out by the right foot, the other four notes only being played by the left foot. Otherwise proceed as before.

Beginning with this D major scale it is necessary to be especially watchful that the knees are kept together, and the feet also, very closely. This will make the work not only more exact, but easier as well. So in the scale of E the feet march along side by side touching each other all the time.

PEDAL GLISSANDO

When the scale of B is reached a new procedure is demanded to permit of passing legato from F♯ to G♯ in the ascending scale, A♯ to G♯ descending. This is *glissando*, which may, therefore, fitly be considered here.

Glissando on the pedal is used with frequency in four fields, namely in passing: (1) from a black key to a white; (2) from a black key to a black; (3) from a white key to a white; (4) from a white key to a black.

(1) In passing from a black key to a white, as in this passage for the right foot:

the only way to play legato is to slide from C♯ to D with the toe; this gives you the heel for E, and the toe in position to play the F♯. Incidentally, you must guard against too much clatter of the keys.

(2) In moving from a black key to another black key advance "toeing in," if possible, up with the left foot, down with the right, as this gives you better control of the keys. If the action of the organ is absolutely noiseless, or, frequently, when you are playing full organ, you can slide from one note to the other on the outer edge of the sole of the foot; otherwise, play the first black note with the outer side of the shoe and the second black note with the inner side, moving it over by throwing the heel in quickly:

thus, left foot  but right foot

Occasionally it is necessary to advance "toeing out," instead, as in octave runs when both feet are busy:

(3) and (4) Passing from a white key to a white or from a white key to a black is demanded only in glissando runs, as described at the end of this chapter.

SUBSTITUTION

Another aid to legato playing which is as indispensable to pedal as to manual technique is Substitution. This is of two kinds: I. Substitution of one foot for another; II. Exchange of heel and toe of the same foot.

I. Substitution of one foot for another is necessary to maintain the legato when two extended melodic skips occur in immediate succession, as:

Play low C with the left toe, second C with the right heel, well forward on the key; substitute left toe for right heel and play high C with right toe. Only so can this be played legato. Always, if possible, substitute a heel for a toe, or a toe for a heel; if the heel is placed well forward on the key and the toe of the other foot back of it, there will be no danger of tripping.

II. Exchange of heel and toe of the same foot.

When you find yourself in a position which demands that a white key shall be followed by a black, and for some good and sufficient reason you have played the white key with the toe, it becomes necessary to substitute the heel for the toe on that white key in order that the toe may be set free to play the black key without interrupting the legato.

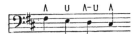

This form of substitution is frequently overdone; organists will sometimes play down a whole scale in this manner. It is well to avoid unnecessary and superfluous use of it, as it can establish itself as a sort of nervous habit.

There is no reason that can be accepted as adequate for breaking the legato in any piece or passage which should be played legato. When, for instance, you are playing an expressive melody and your right foot is occupied with the Swell pedal, do not imagine that you have in this any excuse for permitting the left foot to play a legato passage roughly, or staccato; you can maintain the perfect legato with the left foot, and that not merely in playing adjacent keys, but thirds, fourths and fifths.

When playing a sixth, or anything larger, which the left foot cannot compass alone, bring the right foot down from the Swell pedal for the one extra note; see "Pedal Etude in A," Alkan, in Part II, Section XX.

PLAYING SKIPS OF A THIRD

In order to play thirds on the white keys legato, as in such a passage as

when the right toe depresses middle C swing the heel over D to E, turning the foot slightly in order to have the full benefit of its arch in avoiding D; then use the heel which is depressing E as a pivot on which to swing the toe over F to G; then use the toe which is depressing G as a pivot to swing the heel over A to B.

SEQUENTIAL PEDALING

A point of general importance in pedaling, as indeed in manual technique as well, is to take care that when sequential passages occur in the music the pedaling — or fingering — shall be sequential also. Even though there may be some awkward spots it is worth while to persist in this as it is much easier and more satisfactory in the end.

EXTENDED PEDAL GLISSANDO

Extended pedal glissando has been made possible by the modern pedal keyboard. When it is necessary to execute a run on the white notes of the pedals with the right foot, draw the foot rapidly over the keys, playing on the ball of the foot if moving up the keyboard, on the outer side if moving down. Reverse this procedure for the left foot.

When this run includes both black and white notes, as the scale of E♭, for example,

pull the foot with heel first E♭ to D, D to C, movements with which you are already familiar; at C turn the foot with the toe *in* and play *up* on the black note B♭. A♭, G, F, call for only familiar movements; then toe in again and play *up* on E♭. In passing from a white key to a black in a glissando run it is necessary always to raise the toe sufficiently to permit it to slide up on the black key from the white, pulling the foot in and out in order to reach the keys. This is, of course, impossible on an old-fashioned, straight, stiff keyboard.

Going back up the scale of E♭ the movements will be reversed: E♭, F, G, are played pulling the heel first with the toe turned in; to reach A♭ turn the foot around, with the toe *out* slide to B♭; turn the heel out and slide to C and D with the toe in; slide to E♭ with the heel in, toe out.

Sometimes in such runs, as in the scale of E major, for example. it will be found advantageous to effect the glissando on the white notes with the heel; see Part II, Section XX.

TOUCHES OTHER THAN LEGATO

The other organ touches besides the legato, namely, I. Non-legato, Semi-detached, or Brillante; II. Marcato; III. Staccato, are employed on the pedal as on the manuals, in the same kinds of passages and with the same effects. They are controlled from the ankle. Studies in these touches will be found in Part II, Sections X, XI.

CHAPTER IV

PART-PLAYING, INCLUDING THE PLAYING OF HYMNS

TREATMENT OF REPEATED NOTES

In part-playing when a note is immediately repeated in the same part the first note is given half its value; this applies to both inner and outer voices and to the pedal, and holds no matter how many times a note is repeated. This rule applies also, of course, to the playing of a melody.

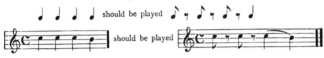

If the repeated note is a very long note, occupying a whole measure, give the first note three-quarters of its value.

This is a point in which organ playing differs utterly from piano playing. On the piano, even though the damper be raised from the key and the wire is still vibrating you can keep on striking the key and effect repetition of the tone. But on the organ there must be interruption of the tone in order to cause it to sound again; to obtain the effect of a repeated note there must be a certain period of silence. The general principle, therefore, is to give the first of two soundings of a note half its value. This must be done even in absolutely legato playing. Too many players do not repeat the note, but tie it over, with resultant destruction of all definite melody and rhythm. The habit of not allowing sufficient time between repeated notes became so general that Widor, in desperation, in the second edition of his symphonies, instead of writing two whole notes in succession wrote the first note as a double-dotted half note followed by an eighth rest:

This same principle applies to violin playing, and the neglect of it was so general that composers for violin finally ceased writing, for example, a series of repeated eighth notes, staccato, and write instead sixteenth notes followed by sixteenth rests:

When the same note occurs again immediately not in the same part but in another part, that is to say, when two voices exchange a note, these repeated notes are tied, and not separated.

Here the C is really *held*, but as it appears in a new part it takes on new character and sounds as though it were played again, yet gives a beautiful legato effect that cannot be obtained on any other instrument.

21

(a)
Andante

J. Durand,
"Feuillet d' Album," Op. 4

(b) Such a phrase as

is played ... while ... is played

A combination of both, as ... is played

Close observance of the principles of separating repeated notes, with all others played legato, will, in most cases, make clear the phrasing of Bach and other contrapuntal music. If you will play these measures from the Bach "Fugue in G minor" according to these principles you will find that the theme naturally phrases itself:

Written

BACH

Played

HYMN-PLAYING

These principles of part-playing should be carefully observed in the playing of hymns. Play a hymn as you would the sustained movement of a sonata, exercising the same care in separating notes repeated in the same part and connecting with perfect legato all others. Thus the tune "Hamburg":

HAMBURG

L. MASON
Adapted from a Gregorian Chant

King - doms and thrones to . God be - long; Crown him, ye na - tions, in your song:

His won-drous name and pow'r re - hearse; His hon - ors shall en - rich your verse.

Should be played as follows :

Some inconsistent practices have prevailed in hymn-playing which would not be tolerated in other part-playing, and which are responsible in a very considerable measure for weak and indefinite congregational singing; the repeated notes are all tied together indiscriminatingly so that the playing is without pulse, and the congregation does not know with assurance just where it is singing. This is most destructive, of course, when the notes are tied in the soprano part, as in such a hymn as "Sun of my Soul," for which see Part II, Section VII. Indefiniteness and the resultant uncertainty are fatal to strong, confident, universal participation in the hymn-singing.

The only exception to the strict application of the rules of part-playing to hymn-playing may be made if the organist has to play a Gospel Hymn of the least musical type, in which identically the same chord is repeated many times in quick succession. To avoid an impression of extreme commonplaceness he may sustain the inner voices and repeat the outer ones only, thus giving the rhythm decidedly but lending greater dignity to the hymn. It is also worth remembering that hymns having anything of this character should not be played too fast in church, but should be taken legato, slower tempo, and seriously, to endow them with all the dignity possible. It is always the organist's privilege to exercise forethought and care to make the musical part of the service as worthy and impressive as possible.

ANNOUNCING A HYMN

There are three principal ways of announcing a hymn: (a) It may be played through on the manuals on the foundation stops of the organ; (b) it may be given out with the three upper parts on the manuals and the bass part on the pedal; (c) the soprano may be played as a solo on one manual with the alto and tenor on another and the bass part on the pedal. An illustration of each of these methods will be found in Part II, Section VII.

ACCOMPANYING CONGREGATIONAL SINGING

In playing a hymn for congregational singing the three upper parts are taken on the manuals, the lowest part on the pedal. This pedal part should be played where it is written, although, occasionally, in a hymn sung by a large congregation it is permissible to drop an octave to give greater sonority, especially on a small organ. This should never be done, however, where it would destroy the outline of the melody of the bass, as, for instance, when it would run below the pedal keyboard and necessitate a leap back in the opposite direction.

For accompanying a fair-sized congregation on a large organ, Mezzo Forte—Great (Diapasons 8', Flutes 8', 4') with full Swell and Choir coupled will supply about the volume of tone necessary; a larger congregation will demand greater volume, but this is about a fair minimum, and you can rarely drop below it if you expect to have your congregation sing. It is well worth while for the organist to take considerable pains to estimate this point with respect to his organ, church edifice, and congregation, as good, hearty congregational singing may be vastly encouraged, or it may be killed, by the organist's manner of accompanying the hymns.

The organist must gain and keep the confidence of the congregation in his hymn-playing and never abuse it by dropping suddenly to a *pianissimo* and leaving them stranded, unsupported. You have only to sit in the congregation and listen when an organist plays a hymn with exaggerated effects, to note that the people around you who have been joining heartily in the singing take alarm when the organ almost drops out in a *pianissimo* so that they hear their own voices, and stop singing. "Expression" in hymn-playing, in accompanying a congregation, is to be indulged in only with the most careful discrimination. You must lead and the singers must always be confident of your support. Of course, you do play the National Anthem and "Abide with me" with different quantity and quality of tone, and, instinctively, congregations sing them so; the fiery Reeds are called upon to stir enthusiastic response in a ringing, patriotic or brilliant hymn, while the calm Diapason tone is better suited to the mood of a quiet, contemplative hymn. It is the sudden change in the middle of a hymn that is disastrous.

This does not apply to a church in which it is the custom for the members of the congregation to meet for practice in hymn-singing; under such conditions the organist has rehearsed his effects beforehand, so that he can accompany as he would a choir. Such churches are still, however, very greatly in the minority.

TIME ALLOWANCE BETWEEN VERSES AND LINES

Do not neglect to give your congregation time enough to take a breath between verses—not too much time, however, or they lose their enthusiasm. It is not desirable, under ordinary circumstances, to play an interlude between verses. A most effective finish for each verse of a hymn is to continue to hold the last chord — which choir and congregation are singing — with the right hand and pedal on the Great its full value, then, as you signal your choir (with a nod) to stop singing, take the same chord on the Swell with the Swell box closed, with the other hand and without any break whatever.

In order to avoid such a break it will quite frequently be found necessary to hold, say, the Soprano and Alto, Tenor and Bass with the thumb and fifth finger of each hand to permit the second and fourth fingers of each hand to be in position over the corresponding keys on the Swell, ready to play the chord which is to be held between verses.

The use of this finish for each verse of a hymn does away with a wait which is embarrassing if nothing is going on, and is not disagreeable as is the sustaining of one pedal note, which is a quite common practice. The effect is quite that of an echo of the last chord. One of its greatest advantages is that the moment you release this chord on the Swell the congregation takes notice that a new verse is to begin and will sing the very first word with the choir, instead of straggling in on the second or third.

It is not only between the verses of a hymn that a congregation needs time to breathe; there must be some concession at the end of each line. In his "The Complete Organist" Harvey Grace complains: "Too many of us try to take our congregations by the scruff of the neck, so to speak, and haul them from line to line of a hymn tune as if the most vital thing in music were its division into bars of equal length.... When Debussy gives us such a rhythmical scheme as a bar of four beats followed by one of five, we say, 'How delightfully elastic!' When our congregation gives us pretty much the same thing we shoot out our reeds and say, 'No, you don't!' " This elasticity does not by any means involve loss of rhythm. The hymn may be thought of as built of curving lines, not angles; its rhythm swings like a pendulum; a pause may be made at the end of a line, like the pause at the end of a swing of a pendulum, without breaking the rhythm, although a pause which is not well calculated will undoubtedly do so.

MAINTAINING THE TEMPO

When a congregation is dragging the tempo play slightly staccato, or marcato; if you continue to drone along legato they will sing more and more slowly. Play slightly staccato, and very slightly in advance, but not much, as you must not disconcert them by running away from them; unconsciously they will quicken the tempo.

THE AMEN

If you use an "Amen" after the hymn do not get into the habit of playing it with a reduced body of tone out of all proportion to that used for the hymn itself. It may be, perhaps it usually is, a very little softer; but an Amen is not inherently a sad thing, although too often, after a cheerful, even triumphant hymn it takes on a tone of mournful resignation.

ANGLICAN CHANTING

Full directions for Anglican Chanting are to be found in the new Hymnal of the Protestant Episcopal Church; they are, therefore, not included here.

CHAPTER V

CHANGING FROM ONE MANUAL TO ANOTHER
PLAYING ON TWO MANUALS SIMULTANEOUSLY WITH ONE HAND

A. CHANGING MANUALS — LEGATO

To pass from one manual to another for the sake of a change of color:

I. When you are playing a melody, or any one part, and want to drop, for example, from Swell to Great for another part, pull the hand *out* on the Swell keyboard so that the finger playing the last note on that keyboard will be on the edge of the key, and drop the other fingers to the manual below, to the keys on which they are to play.

If you wish to pass upwards, as from Great to Swell, the process must be reversed; shove the finger playing the last note *in* on the keyboard. It is an advantage in this case to have the thumb play the last note if possible.

When in passing from a lower to a higher manual the thumb plays the last note, or when in going from a higher to a lower manual it plays the first note, it is possible to move legato not only to the next manual but to the second above or below, that is to say, it is possible to play the illustration just above on Choir and Swell.

II. When you are playing chords and wish to pass from an upper to a lower manual draw all the fingers to the very edge of the keys and drop them. If you are playing a chord of only three notes on the upper manual, drop the remaining two fingers over their notes below while you are still playing the chord above, so that half the work of transference may be already done:

In passing from a lower to a higher manual reverse this process; this is frequently demanded in playing hymns for congregational singing, especially the chord on the Swell which serves as interlude between verses.

One of the differences between a careful legato player and a careless player lies in the fact that the latter does not exercise the foresight or take the trouble necessary to prepare his fingers for such transferences, with the result that roughnesses and breaks always appear in his playing.

When you are obliged to move from a chord on the Choir to one on the Swell be careful to take off all the notes on the lower manual at once. The hand naturally moves up little finger first, so that the thumb is apt to hang on to its note after the other notes of the chord have been released, causing blurring.

B. Changing Manuals — Staccato.

In passing from one manual to another with staccato chords swiftness, mental as well as physical, is the prime requisite. Your eyes must travel ahead of your fingers. In the following section of Guilmant's "Caprice in B Flat," for example, you cannot finish playing the chord on the Great before you look at the keys on the Swell on which you are to play the next chord:

It is necessary to cultivate the habit of having the eyes anticipate the movements of the hands and prepare the way for them; if you form the conception of the chord *as it is to be played, and where,* your hands will automatically assume the position of playing it. When it is started on its way look ahead to the next one.

Playing on Two Manuals simultaneously with the Same Hand

A melody may be played with some of the fingers of one hand on one manual, and a counter melody with the thumb and other fingers of the same hand on another manual, leaving the other hand free for the accompaniment:

SERENADE

PIERNÉ

Occasionally it is necessary to employ all the fingers of both hands on an upper manual and to play the melody on a lower manual with both thumbs, as in the "Rondo Capriccio" by Lemare:

R.H. Fingers on Swell : Voix Cel., Lieblich, Vox Humana, Lieb. Bourdon 16 ft., Trem.

Both thumbs on Gt. (Flute 8 ft.), coup. to Sw.

L.H. Fingers on Sw.

Pedal (soft 16 ft., 8ft.).

CHAPTER VI

ADAPTING PIANO ACCOMPANIMENTS TO THE ORGAN

The organist constantly finds it necessary to adapt to his instrument piano accompaniments to solos and choral numbers and piano reductions of orchestral scores of oratorios. Accompaniments as printed are apt to be unorganistic in the following respects particularly:

1. REPEATED CHORDS

Numerous repetitions of the same chord in quick succession are not suited to the organ. It is necessary to modify the manner of playing them, as follows: repeat several notes of the chord in order to give the rhythm desired, but sustain others in order to give more body to the tone, and to bring out what melody there may be in one of the parts, usually the upper; as in this phrase from Faure's "The Palms":

Sometimes, however, the notes must be played exactly as written, as in the accompaniment to the following recitative for Bass in Haydn's "Creation," which is meant to suggest the buzzing of insects:

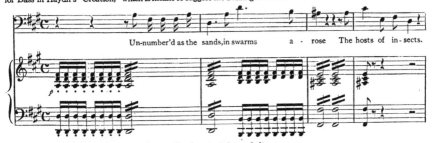

This is the case only when the text or the emotional content demands it.

2. ARPEGGIOS

Arpeggios made up of single notes or of chords are ineffective and thin on the organ if played as they are written. Therefore, (a) when playing on one manual an ascending and descending arpeggio of single notes, the lower notes, or a proportion of them, are sustained after being taken in the ascending arpeggio until they are played again in the descending:

(b) When playing a long, rapid, ascending and descending arpeggio on a Flute on one manual let it be accompanied by the corresponding chord sustained on a second manual, in order to give body of tone, as the arpeggio alone gives too thin an effect. The sustaining chord must, of course, be softer than the arpeggio in order not to overwhelm it.

Played:
Moaerato con grazia
Ch. Fl.

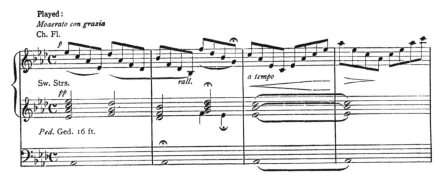

When the arpeggio possesses the character of a melody, however, this effect of tenuousness may be desirable, together with the resultant distinct enunciation of the different notes; or a light, delicate effect of "dropping" single, detached notes may be required. This is exemplified in the accompaniment to the Tenor aria "In Native Worth," in Haydn's "Creation":

(c) A form of arpeggio of very frequent occurrence which is unorganistic is the repetition of the arpeggios which are within the stretch of one hand. Sustain the corresponding chord on one manual, and play the arpeggios on a different manual, or on the same an octave higher:

The procedure in playing an arpeggio of chords is the same as in playing one of single notes:

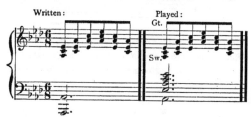

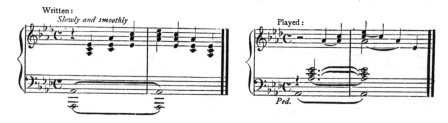

If manifestly intended to be played as detached harp-like chords it is

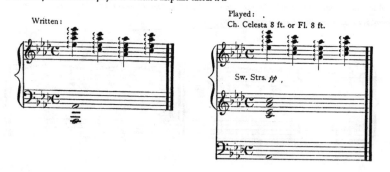

3. Extreme Skips

Skipping from one extreme of the keyboard to the other is a proceeding quite out of keeping with the nature of the organ as an instrument. Quite frequently in a piano accompaniment a chord taken on the lower section of the keyboard is followed immediately by one played on the upper part of the keyboard, and this figure is repeated several times. Played on the organ exactly as written it produces an effect almost ridiculous. This is avoided by continuing to hold the lower chord with the left hand and pedal while you are playing the upper chord with the right hand:

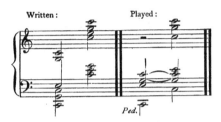

4. Passages with Upper and Lower Parts widely Separated

Passages in which there is a wide discrepancy in range between the upper and lower parts, that is to say, in which the upper and lower parts are widely separated, the one lying very high and the other low, are far from satisfactory if played on the organ as they are written. It is necessary to fill in the middle part:

5. Chords in Low Register

When chords are written full in low register the effect on the organ is apt to be too thick and muddy. They should be transferred to an upper register; usually it will suffice to play them an octave higher than they are written, giving the bass part on the pedal:

6. TREMOLO CHORDS

When chords appear in the form which in the piano score corresponds to the string tremolo of the orchestra the inner voices should be sustained while the outer keys are depressed alternately in rapid succession to produce the tremolo. The necessity for making this adjustment arises most frequently in *agitato* passages in oratorios. If all notes are given the tremolo the effect is utterly unorganistic; if all notes are sustained the intense excitement of the passage is deadened and its dramatic quality lost. A good example of this is found in the accompaniment to the Tenor solo "The Sorrows of Death" in Mendelssohn's "Hymn of Praise":

Sometimes, but *rarely*, when the tremolo is in the bass, it is effective to let the pedal trill on the bass note and the half tone below:

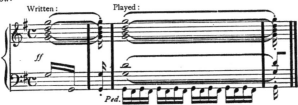

7. ROLLED CHORDS

In playing rolled chords, sustain every note as you play it until after you have played the last note of the chord, then release them all with downward motion. It is essential to fix in the mind this conception of releasing them with downward motion or you will certainly let the lower ones off first, giving the chord a small, thin tone; the bottom will drop out of it.

RELEASE OF CHORDS

Just here we may note in passing that chords should be released downward, but so rapidly that the hearer is not conscious of any one note hanging on after any other. Even a poor downward release will be less noticeable than the overhang of an upper note, which is certain to sound thin and insistent. With practice the student can secure a downward release which is clean and satisfying. If the acoustics of the building are perfect a chord in which all notes are released at exactly the same moment gives the most brilliant effect.

VOLUME OF ACCOMPANIMENT

In accompanying vocal or instrumental solos or choral numbers beware of playing too loud. Give enough organ to furnish support but never enough to interfere with the predominance of the solo part.

It is well to remember not to keep the Swell box closed for too long a period when accompanying, as it makes the accompaniment vague and indefinite; the singer will be able to hear the accompaniment better, and will have a clearer, more distinct impression of the pitch if you use stops that will permit you to keep it at least partly open.

REGISTRATION OF ORCHESTRAL ACCOMPANIMENTS

Some knowledge of orchestration is of great value in accompanying; it will often enable the accompanist to make a more reasonable and fitting choice of colors for the background of the accompaniment, and of stops (instruments) to bring out counter melodies.

For example: in the accompaniment of "It is Enough," from Mendelssohn's "Elijah," the accompanying chords originally scored for Strings in the orchestra are best given to the Strings on the organ, while the obbligato, originally scored for Violoncello, is best brought out by the Cornopean (or Gamba Celeste), with which the Tremulant will be used, as the cello player invariably employs the vibrato throughout this number.

But the organist who is not a master of orchestration may be guided aright by his knowledge of his own instrument. First of all, he will be careful to use one of the stops of greatest effectiveness in the particular range of the melody to be played. Thus, in the range of the obbligato of "It is Enough" a Diapason, String, or Reed must be chosen, the Flute being too dull entirely to be used in that register. Secondly, he will consider the color desired, basing his choice of stops on the character of the text and of the music which should reflect and interpret that text. This melody "It is Enough" is in minor, warm, throbbing, the last passionate cry of despair. A Diapason will, therefore, be too cool; a String will be much better, and may be used if an organ lacks a suitable Reed; but the stop that best voices this emotion is a Reed, the Cornopean, with the Tremulant.

In the middle section the number changes character. The obbligato drops out and the accompaniment works up on the foundation stops in the usual manner to full Swell. Just here, note that these repeated chords should be played as written, for impassioned, dramatic effect. With the return of the original melody the original registration will be again employed.

"IT IS ENOUGH."

Again, in accompanying a soprano singing such a number as "With Verdure Clad," from Haydn's "Creation," which is a cool, rippling melody in Flute range, use pure Flute tone — 8' and 4' Flutes on the Swell with 8' Flute on the Choir or Great, for the short obbligato bits. The brief *agitato* interlude and the vocal section corresponding call for Strings.

A distinguished bass asked me recently why young organists almost invariably accompany him on Flutes, which give him no support and do not blend with his voice. Flutes can very seldom be used in directly accompanying a bass voice, although most valuable for color relief in the interludes.

String tone and Diapason tone are the backbone of accompanying. The heavy Reeds are used for stirring, martial, triumphant passages, or are added to other stops for climax; the lighter Reeds, as the Oboe, Clarinet, Cornopean, etc., are used for obbligato bits, as we have seen in the above consideration of "It is Enough."

Good accompanying demands the closest attention to the solo (or choral) part, as well as to the accompaniment. Your part may be rather colorless and uninteresting but it must be played with all the *verve* that may lie in the vocal part. Moreover, it is necessary to be very wide awake, in closest touch with the singer, and on the alert to anticipate every nuance of color, volume, or rhythm. The singer should never be obliged to carry the organ and organist as well as the song. You can enhance immeasurably the beauty of a solo or choral number, or you can seriously detract from it, even spoil it altogether, by poor accompanying or contradictory registration.

CHAPTER VII

THE MANIPULATION OF THE SWELL PEDAL

The technique of the Swell pedal means, first of all, perfect command of a gradual crescendo and diminuendo, with no sudden outbursts or dampenings of sound — a nicety of control which is gained only by much careful practice. The exception to this is the sforzando passage, or the sudden crescendo for the sake of accent; this matter of accent by means of the Swell pedal is considered in Chapter VIII.

The same perfect command of carefully graduated movement is essential also in the use of the Crescendo Pedal, an illustration of which will be found in Guilmant's "Marche Réligieuse," Part II, Section XIX.

In some cases, when you want only a slight crescendo and diminuendo and a quick one, it is necessary to play on the middle of the Swell, as it were; that is to say, not to close or open the Swell entirely. Mechanically, this means using the middle contacts only of the set of electrical contacts by which the modern Swell is operated. The effect in the following passage from the Bach "Fugue in D minor" is absurd if you go from the tightly closed box to the wide-open box, as the growth in the volume of sound is too great for the time allowance; the crescendo should begin with the Swell box one-quarter open and finish with it three-quarters open.

This is a point of great importance in playing accompaniments, when effects must be very delicately calculated.

It is not always necessary to have the foot on the Swell pedal in order to move it; very often it can be moved without letting go the pedal note the foot is occupied in playing. For instance, when the left foot is holding lower E and the right foot middle E and it is necessary to open or close the Swell box, hold E with the heel and open the Swell box with the toe of the same foot. Two adjacent pedals may be manipulated at the same time with one foot; they may be opened and closed together by putting the foot half on one and half on the other; or, one may be opened and the other closed almost simultaneously by using the toe to open one and the heel to close the other.

BALANCING TWO SWELL PEDALS

When you are playing two melodies on different manuals the manual which has the important part must have its Swell box opened; as soon as the other manual assumes a strain of first importance the former is subdued by closing its Swell box, and this one is made to advance into prominence by opening its Swell box wider. This is a matter of proportion, as in singing a duet, and will require careful study that the balance may be perfectly adjusted and the nuances not only proper but musical.

Sw. Ob. or Sw. Eng. Hr. 16 ft., Ob. 8 ft., Strs. 8 ft.
Ch. Clar. or Ch. Eng. Hr. 16 ft., Orch. Ob. 8 ft., Quint., Strs. 8 ft., 16 ft.

LISZT

This is of constant importance in playing a melody with accompaniment; occasionally the accompaniment takes on increased interest, so that it may even become of greater consequence than the melody; it should then be brought out into the prominence it deserves by means of the Swell pedal. Too often an accompaniment to a melody is permitted to degenerate into a mere colorless background, occasionally too loud, more frequently too soft, and with its points of character and interest all unnoticed. The Swell pedal controlling the accompaniment should be in use almost as much as the one controlling the melody. When you are playing such a melody with accompaniment imagine yourself, for instance, a violinist and at the same time a pianist accompanying that violinist, and suit your accompaniment to the solo.

CHANGE OF TONE QUALITY BY MEANS OF THE SWELL PEDAL

1. To pass from one quality of tone to another without change of manual, as from String to Flute tone, draw the Flutes in the Choir and the Strings of the same strength in the Swell, couple Swell to Choir and play on the Choir. The change of tone quality may then be effected by the use of the Swell pedal: begin with the Choir open, Swell closed; gradually close the Choir and open the Swell.

This can be done on a one-manual organ, or on an organ in which Diapasons, Flutes, Strings, and Reeds each have a separate Swell box; or, as in Dr. Audsley's specifications, where two manual divisions of the organ are in

40

separate boxes though played from the same manual; or, what is more common, where stops from one manual are borrowed on another.

2. Smooth and gradual transition from one color to another is a matter of skillful manipulation of the Swell pedal.

3. Different qualities of tone color can be made to melt into one another like dissolving views on the stereopticon. For instance, to change from String tone on the Swell to Flute tone on the Choir: while the chord is being held on the Strings of the Swell with the Swell box open, take the Flute tone on the Choir with the Swell box closed; if you take it note after note from the bottom upward it will come on even more gradually; then slowly close the Swell; when that is closed, slowly open the Choir; then release the notes on the Swell one by one from the top downward.

CHAPTER VIII

ACCENT

The assertion that no accent is possible on the organ is absurd, and its effect in application would be deadly. It is not obtained by increased pressure, however, but in various other ways.

1. Accent may be obtained by the sudden partial opening and closing of the Swell pedal. The process may be described as "circling the note" with the Swell pedal; the note comes in the exact center of the two movements of opening and closing, which must both be executed at a high rate of speed. The motion is a double action of the ankle (toe and heel), the same motion as that of the wrist in cracking a whip.

2. Accent may be obtained by holding back from the attack of a note or chord a barely appreciable trifle; this implies a pause which may be infinitesimal, but which increases in length as demanded by the tempo or the requirements of dramatic effect or climax. This pause catches the attention of the ear, focusses that attention on the particular note or chord, and gives a perfect effect of accent. The slighter the separation the lighter the accent. The effect will be better realized if such a passage as the following from Liszt's "Fantasia and Fugue on B-A-C-H" is played through smoothly, legato, without accent; then played through again with a slight holding back before the chord or chords which constitute the final climax of the phrase — holding back slightly before each chord but a little longer before the last one that it may be unmistakably the climax. Unaccented, the compelling virility and sweeping power of even this splendid phrase are lost.

This device is not peculiar to the organ, but is employed by players on every instrument, and by orchestral conductors. One of the secrets of Weingartner's power as a conductor was the manner in which he would work up the orchestra in a gradual accelerando and crescendo, then, just before the climax, hold back in a sometimes barely appreciable pause, upon which the climax came with seemingly tremendous force.

3. Accent may be obtained by holding a note a barely appreciable fraction longer than its face value — *marcato* or *tenuto*,—an effect which is also illustrated in the preceding example. As the matter of accent is so closely bound up with rhythm, see also Chapter IX, "Rhythm."

41

CHAPTER IX

RHYTHM

The ultimate element of style in organ playing is rhythm; it is truly, as Berlioz said, "the pulsing life blood of music." It is not easy to impart or to acquire it; indeed the assertion is often made that it is impossible; that rhythm, like color, is a gift, not an acquirement. There are, however, points which may be mastered, and some suggestions may aid the student in gaining control of his own feeling for rhythm, in which direction training is necessary even for those most highly endowed by nature.

An important detail which may be mentioned at the very outset is the necessity of always adjusting yourself before beginning a number; take an extra second to adapt yourself mentally and emotionally to the number you are about to play; put yourself into its mood, its tempo, and its rhythm. Then never "let go" again during the number; be mentally ready beforehand for each change and climax within it.

Holding Steadily to the Beat

The first essential in developing a sense of rhythm is the cultivation of the power to hold to the steady, implacable, unvarying recurrence of the beat. The careless, lazy player lets it drag, and slip, and become indefinite, and the temperamental player hurries, and breaks, or unreasonably varies it. This mastery of steady observance of the beat is especially difficult of accomplishment in crescendo passages without accelerando, or in diminuendo passages without ritardando; the student of rhythm should learn to build up such passages and permit them to subside again very gradually, and with absolute steadiness.

Perfect Proportion in Changing Tempo

Having acquired the ability to hold steadily to the beat in all kinds of passages, the next step is to learn to increase the pace, to play accelerando passages without destroying the regularity of the pulse beats; that is to say, to move *in proportion* through the change of tempo, taking off exactly the same amount of time from each successive beat. For example, in such a passage as

42

from Guilmant's "Marche Réligieuse," Part II, Section XII, page 171, take off, say, one-ninetieth of the value of 1, one-eightieth of the value of 2, one-seventieth of the value of 3, one-sixtieth of the value of 4, and so on. The figures are not given as a statement of actual physical measurement, but to illustrate the absolute regularity and proportion of the speed progression. The rhythm will not be maintained if you vary instead, say, from one-ninetieth to one-sixtieth, to one-forty-fifth, and so on. The procedure in a ritardando passage is, of course, the reverse of this.

SIGNIFICANCE OF ACCELERANDO

Just here it may not be amiss to note that the indication *accel.* is too often interpreted as calling for a sudden, immediate, quite violent quickening of the tempo. This is not its significance; but rather "accelerate," do not jump. It implies a very gradual quickening of the tempo from that point on, causing it to move steadily, in perfect proportion, faster and faster as it proceeds, to the end of the passage. *Piu mosso* is the term employed to indicate a sudden quickening of the tempo.

Too frequently are the crescendo and accelerando regarded as inseparable companions, as are, likewise, the diminuendo and ritardando, and monotony of style results. A crescendo is sometimes more effective and impressive when accompanied by a ritard, while a piquant or humorous turn may be given by the association of a diminuendo and an accelerando.

DICKINSON
From Scherzo, "Storm King" Symphony

Having gained control of steady rhythmic movement the next desideratum is to free yourself from the metronomic shackles with which you have willingly bound yourself, to enjoy liberty in the handling of rhythm and the "give and take" of all truly rhythmic movement. Rhythmic freedom never means indulgence in the license of illogical hurry or delay, or the placing of accent where it destroys the identity and coherence of the theme. The tempo may be varied within the compass of one bar so that the ritardando exactly balances the accelerando, and the time value of the bar is not altered; the rhythm marches right along, the initial pulse of each measure beating with perfect regularity.

Rhythm is varied with two main objects: (1) for purposes of dynamics; (2) for purposes of expression.

44

AGOGICS

(1) When this variation is made for purposes of dynamics, that is to say, to give the *effect* of increasing or diminishing the tone, it is spoken of as agogics, and the accent obtained as agogical accent. In such a phrase as

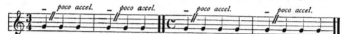

the slight hold on the first note of each bar causes a loss of time which must be made up by the quickening of the following notes in the measure; the time allowance for the whole is not changed, but accent is obtained, the rhythm is defined, and the theme is distinctly enunciated.

Longer measures necessitate secondary accents as well.

That such proper agogics are essential in preserving the identity of a theme may be more fully realized if you play a group of notes with the accent at various different points in the phrase; the change in the position of the accent changes the theme entirely.

This is most important in enunciating contrapuntal themes, as in the Bach "Fugue in A minor," or his "Fantasia in G," from which these passages are taken:

The organist frequently plays on organs in divisions of which it is impossible to obtain much variation of volume of tone, as little of the organ is under mechanical control; the effect of changing volume and accent he desires will be obtained through the application of these principles. He also makes use of them when, in playing full organ, for example, he desires an *effect* of accent and increased or diminished volume of sound without any actual enlarging or dampening of the tone.

TEMPO RUBATO

(2) The variation of rhythm for the sake of expression is known as *tempo rubato*. The same principle of balance of the ritardando and accelerando apply, although not necessarily within the confines of one measure; the passage may be several bars in length. This *tempo rubato* is employed also in playing the cadenza or recitative passages such as occur frequently in the works of the older composers as Frescobaldi, Froberger, Gabrieli, Bach, or of Liszt, Chopin, and modern orchestral writers; the general principle is: start very slowly, accelerate very gradually to rapid tempo at the middle point, then slow down very gradually, ending in the tempo in which you began.

A word of caution may be spoken against always exaggerating effects. Do not always indulge in a rushing accelerando or in an excessive holding-back for a ritardando. By so doing you spoil the possibility of an intensely dramatic effect when it might be secured by the employment of just such an accelerando or ritardando. Some composers endeavor to make known their desires in this respect by the indication *"poco rit.,"* but the *"poco"* is often ignored. A famous French composer once said to me, "I would frequently like a slight holding-back, but I do not dare indicate it on the music, as it would almost invariably be interpreted as a full-sized ritard." This slight holding-back is especially important in playing Fugues, when it serves to call the attention of the hearers to the entrances of the theme which would otherwise slip in unnoticed, but where the introduction of a real ritard would interfere with the flow of the composition, and, in constant recurrence, would prove very wearing.

CLIMAX

To work up a climax most effectively, combine a very gradual crescendo and accelerando until just before the point of climax, then hold back a barely appreciable instant and then attack the final chord *fff*; it will seem to come with tremendous force. Or, just before the point of climax hold back an instant and take the final three or four chords *marcato*, and with a slight ritard.

RESTS

In any study of rhythm as much attention must be paid to rests as to notes. They have just the same value as the notes whose allotted time they fill with silence, and they must be treated as fully as significant in the interpretation of a composition. Inattention to this point is a frequent fault which destroys the melodic line and ruins the rhythm. Beethoven said, "The rest is the most eloquent thing in music."

DRAWING STOPS WITHOUT LOSS OF RHYTHM

Frequently the flow of rhythm is interrupted by the player drawing stops. Do not draw stops while a note or chord is sounding except on an accent either real or metrical. Musical feeling is offended when stops are drawn in the middle of a beat with a resultant disastrous change in color and volume. Do not stop playing to draw a stop, and, above all, do not hang on to one note or chord long past its appointed time. It is most unfortunate for a player to break the rhythm and utterly destroy the flow of the melody by holding on to some one chord while he draws stops, or even makes up his mind what stops to draw. When it is necessary to make an intricate change of stops on both sides of the console and in the shortest possible space of time do not let your eyes cling to the chord you are playing until it is ended and then look for your stops. Let your eyes anticipate your hands; while your hands are still on the keys look at the stops you are about to draw and get into your mind their relation to one another so that the instant your hands are free you are *ready* to draw the stops.

THE CHIEF FACTORS IN THE DESTRUCTION OF RHYTHM

In brief, the chief factors in the destruction of rhythm are (1) changing stops in the wrong place; (2) holding on to a note or chord beyond its true time value in order to change the registration; (3) ignoring the time value of rests; (4) changing color too frequently and thereby breaking up the outlines of a composition; (5) failure to separate repeated notes; (6) unsteadiness and indefiniteness due to carelessness, or laziness, on the one hand, or to uncontrolled interest and excitement on the other. The organist must always be on the alert lest he slip at any time into one of these pitfalls which will destroy the vibrant, pulsing life of his music; constant care for the cultivation of the sense of rhythm and for its transmission will bring its reward in the mastery of the most elusive yet greatest fascination inherent in musical movement.

CHAPTER X

THE PLAYING OF ORNAMENTS

Although most modern composers write out their ornaments in full it is necessary for the student to understand the ornamental signs in order to interpret correctly the works of Bach and his predecessors. Instruction as to how to play most of those used by Bach is to be found in the little book which the master himself compiled for his son Wilhelm Friedemann; it was begun at Cöthen in 1720 when the boy was nine years old.

1. Trill. 2. Mordent. 3. Trill and Mordent. 4. Cadence. 5. Double Cadence.

6. Double Cadence. 7. Double Cadence and Mordent. 8. Double Cadence and Mordent. 9. Double Cadence and Mordent.

10. Rising Accent or Appoggiatura. 11. Falling Accent or Appoggiatura. 12. Accent and Mordent. 13. Accent and Trill. -14. Accent and Trill.

That his son might proceed at once to the application of the principles of playing ornaments Bach wrote the following little piece, the "Applicatio"; you will note that the right-hand part is written in the old soprano clef and should, therefore, be read a third down.

APPLICATIO   BACH

Besides the graces included in the above the student will meet most frequently of all with the slide:

Trills are also indicated :
tr., $\wedge\wedge\wedge$, t, +, $\wedge\wedge\wedge$.

With Bach and his predecessors the graces were always diatonic in style; they should agree with the scale of the prevailing key. Thus, in the following example from the Bach "Fugue in E minor" the turn involves a whole step downward, to A♮ not A♯.

The definite time value of any ornament must always be observed. This is taken, as a rule, out of the value of the main note. It should also be noted that, for the most part, the graces do not commence on the main note. The appoggiatura without the line takes its time value from the note following; with the line, from the note preceding.

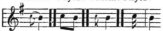

A minute study of all the ornaments used by the early composers and Bach will be found in "The Interpretation of the Music of the Seventeenth and Eighteenth Centuries," by Arnold Dolmetsch, and in "Musical Ornamentation," by Edward Dannreuther.

CHAPTER XI

REGISTRATION AND COLOR

The question of color or registration on the organ is one of the most difficult of all subjects to treat. Color sense is in large measure a gift; fundamentally, the greatest colorists in any art are born, not made. But even those born with this gift have to experiment much to know that they possess it, and have to acquire the technical ability to employ it with the control and restraint which will make its expression emotionally intelligible. Yet in this, one of the most important of all features of organ playing, there is, perhaps, less that can be definitely imparted by one person to another than in any other department; at most a few guide-posts may be set up, a few indications given as to certain resources of the organ and lines of experimentation along which the student can work.

There is nothing more uninteresting than organ playing that is devoid of color; it has a grinding monotony which is deadly. Diapason tone is the foundation of the organ and should be recognized as such by builders and organists alike, but the foundation is by no means the only essential, interesting, or beautiful part of tonal structure any more than it is of architectural. A superstructure of Flutes, Strings, Reeds, is necessary to complete the edifice, with further ornamentation also in the way of exquisite solo stops, Celestes, and so forth, if suitable to the character of the tonal building, and the means are at disposal.

On the other hand, a lavish use of color becomes occasionally a device for covering up lack of technique, for blinding an audience so that it will not realize that there is no real playing behind it. This is shallow, insincere, and tawdry. For this very reason it is usually better for the student to practise on a small organ in which there is less to lure away from the fundamental necessity of obtaining true technical command. Nor need the development of color sense be seriously hampered by the small organ. It should rather sharpen the student's ingenuity to discover how to get the most possible color out of it; it is truly remarkable what color effects can be obtained with an organ of just one manual and only half a dozen stops.

FAMILIES OF TONE COLOR

The families of tone color in the organ are, roughly speaking,

I. Diapason tone; II. (a) Flute tone, (b) Gedackt tone; III. Gemshorn tone; IV. String tone, also called Gamba tone; V. Reed tone, (a) Woodwind tone (Orchestral Reeds), (b) Trumpet tone (Brass, Chorus Reeds).

The stops belonging in each class will be identified by reference to Chapter I.

I. Diapason tone is that of simple, open metal pipes; it should be basic, smooth, sonorous. Its most common use is in broad, full chords, slow-moving, "churchly" passages such as chorales or modal music, or as the foundation of a mass of tone such as one employs in playing contrapuntal music.

In all qualities of tone, however, pitch plays an important part in modifying the color, and the Diapason, which is rich and full in the lower and middle registers, becomes thin and unpleasant in the upper. Flute or String tone is, therefore, more satisfactory in passages of high tessitura.

In a baritone range the Diapason will serve for obbligato or solo purposes.

In the pedal, constant and unrelieved "booming" of the Diapason in *forte* passages may become rather wearing; if you have a Violone stop use that String tone now and then for relief. It may be noted here, in passing, that, in soft passages, instead of using a Bourdon all the time and creating thus an unceasing "pedal buzz," as is often done to excess, it is well to relieve it by the use, now and then, of a String tone, that is to say, a Dulciana or Gamba.

II. Of the Flute family, the Harmonic and Double Flute lend brilliancy of tone; the Concert Flute, Flute d'Amour, and Suabe Flute are mellow; the Concert Flute and Melodia occasionally take on something of the quality of the horn in passages in its register; the Philomela — the largest Flute — is clear, cool, and impersonal in tone quality; the Spitz Flute in combination with the Flute Celeste is a delightful stop for use in accompanying. Flutes are usually the most suitable stops for rapid runs, in any of these combinations: 8' and 4'; 8' and 2'; 8' and 16'; 8', 4', 2'; 8', 4', 16'; 4' and 16'; 4', 2', and 16'; 2' and 16'; and, very rarely, 4' and 2'. Such variety in color may be obtained from Flutes alone.

49

For very high solo passages the Flute is almost invariably the best stop as it is most characteristic in the upper register; in very low range it becomes dull and indefinite.

Arpeggios are generally most effectively given on the Flute when there is no real Celesta in the organ.

Harp-like effects are obtained by playing rolled chords on an 8-foot Flute, or an 8-foot with a soft 16-foot, the latter preferably on another manual coupled, so that it can be made very soft.

Quick-moving, detached chords, such as occur in many *Scherzo* movements, are best brought out on an 8-foot and 4-foot Flute. Flutes respond very quickly, so that the certain crispness desired is most readily obtainable from them.

III. The Gemshorn or Erzähler tone is a cross between a Flute and a String. It may be characterized as charming or piquant. It is useful for soft chords legato in accompanying, or for detached chords with Celesta or 4-foot Flute. The tone is too small and too little distinctive to be of great value for solo use, although occasionally it may be used to bring out a very soft phrase.

IV. The String tone, which on the old-fashioned organs was thin, is in modern organs full, rich, and smooth. This is one of the most useful of the tone families, especially if there are also some Strings of keen, "biting" quality to be used with telling effect in movements instinct with passion and dramatic intensity.

The Strings are also used for the foundation of the quiet movements of sonatas, and in passages in which they would be used by the orchestra.

Because of the definite quality of tone of the Strings, low chords may be best brought out on them, also very high chords, for the reason that they possess the power of being very soft and at the same time distinct and clear cut.

For Solo effects the Gamba Celeste in the violoncello range is the most useful, unless you have a set of orchestral Strings, that is to say, five or six powerful Strings put together to form a String organ, in which case you can bring out a melody in any register.

It is, however, in sustained movements with many parts that the greatest effectiveness of String tone is found.

V. (a) Of the Reeds, the Woodwinds reveal their most beautiful quality in the range of their prototypes in the orchestra. They possess the greatest individuality of any stops, and are therefore most valuable for solo purposes.

The Oboe — or the Flügelhorn, which sometimes takes the place of the Oboe — is best suited to melodies in violin range but may be used satisfactorily for those in cello range when there is no Cornopean in the organ, or when a lighter tone is desired.

The Cornopean with the Tremulant approaches closely the timbre of the violoncello.

The Oboe may be used in sustained soft chords in place of a Vox Humana.

The tone of the Oboe may be said to be "shaded" in the following stops:

1. Flügelhorn, which is richer, fuller, and on a larger scale;

2. Orchestral Oboe, which is thinner and keener;

3. Musette, which is much like the Orchestral Oboe but very much thinner and keener, and the smallest in scale of any Reed;

4. English Horn, which, like its orchestral prototype, has more of an alto quality, with a certain resultant somberness.

In a small organ the place of the Flügelhorn, Orchestral Oboe, Musette, and English Horn is taken by the Oboe; sometimes it will be found possible to use a Clarinet as substitute.

In the organ, as in the orchestra, the French Horn is more often used with the woodwinds than with the brass; moreover, as it is a comparatively light stop in the organ it properly belongs in the former class.

The Clarinet and Bassoon or Fagotto partake of the quality of the orchestral instruments whose name they bear, and are used to obtain the same effects. Both are good solo stops. The Clarinet may be used in rapid runs and in chords in the lower range as well as in melodies.

The Bassoon, or Fagotto, borrowed in the pedal is very useful in defining clearly a soft melody or a bass part.

For an obbligato or solo of pensive character the English Horn is appropriate; for one more striking or brilliant the Orchestral Oboe, which is also suited to melodies of "pastorale" character, as is the Musette. The French Horn will best bring out a smooth, peaceful melody in lower or middle range.- Two melodies, of high and low range respectively, may be effectively contrasted by the use of a Flügelhorn or Orchestral Oboe against a French Horn; if a French Horn is lacking a good clear Diapason will be found very satisfactory.

The Clarinet and French Horn are suited to harmonies in the lower register, the English Horn to those in higher range. The Orchestral Oboe may often be rendered more colorful by the addition of a four-foot Flute; this applies also to the Musette.

The Vox Humana may be used not only as a solo stop — when it is most characteristic in the lower and middle registers — but also in combination with the Strings; it lends a certain fullness and richness of tone quality.

Used principally with the solo Reeds, the Tremulant, which, in spite of all attacks upon it, has always been in use since Bach's day, produces an effect which is well liked and which seems to meet a need for relief from straight tone. Restraint should be exercised in its use, however, as well as in the use of the Vox Humana as a solo stop, or both will lose value and your music will be in danger of becoming over-sentimentalized, even mawkish.

V. (b) Trumpet tone (Brass, Chorus Reeds) is very distinctive, powerful, and assertive. Ringing, jubilant, or fiery, it is best suited to music of triumphant or martial character, fanfare melodies, and heavy detached chords, such as are played by the brass of the orchestra.

In passages of gradually increasing power the Trumpets, Tubas, Trombone, and Bombarde are added to produce a final climax of tremendous impressiveness.

Where there are two Tubas the smaller is usually of so fine and smooth a tone in the modern organ that it can be used interchangeably with the Cornopean for flowing melodies.

A true Tuba Mirabilis is rarely suitable for anything except a single melody which you desire to bring out above full organ, or a passage of climax of the character indicated above. It is generally too large for use in chords with full organ, as it is dominating and obtrudes.

The pedal Reeds are used to bring out melodies or runs against a heavy body of tone or full organ; the 32-foot Bombarde in his organ in Weimar undoubtedly inspired Bach in the creation of some of the majestic pedal passages in his great organ works.

Two valuable artistic assets should never be overlooked: the elements of surprise — not shock, but surprise — and of climax. When working up a tremendous climax reserve if possible some characteristic tone color or some last degree of tone volume such as a Tuba and Bombarde for the climax; do not let them dominate earlier or you sacrifice these two powerful forces of surprise and climax.

Color in interpretation may be obtained through the various families of stops by using them in the following ways:

1. In purity;   2. In combination;   3. In solos with accompaniment;   4. In various color lines weaving in and out, as it were, simultaneously.

COLOR THROUGH USE OF STOPS IN PURITY

1. Using the stops in purity, color may be obtained even on the smallest organ by contrasting the families of tone, as Flutes against Strings in the upper register, or either Flutes or Strings against Diapasons in the lower register. Almost all organs have at least one Reed — an Oboe — which will furnish further contrast to any one of the other three colors.

Even if you have a large organ rich in resources do not neglect the employment of stops in their purity. The combinations of stops, and therefore of varieties of tone color, on the organ are almost incomputable; Dr. Audsley has calculated that about 134,217,700 permutations are possible with an organ of twenty-seven stops. But the organist must never lose sight of the fact that, after all, the most distinctive contrasts in color are obtained through the use of each family of stops by itself; for example, pure Flute tone contrasted with pure String, or single Reed; or a heavy body of all the Reeds on one manual against all the Diapasons on another.

NECESSITY OF THOROUGH KNOWLEDGE OF THE INSTRUMENT TO BE PLAYED

2. Using the stops in combination, the possibilities of color are, as we have seen, almost limitless. Two things there are to which the organist must apply himself in order to ascertain what colors to use in the interpretation of a composition: (a) he must know his organ, and (b) he must study the composition to be interpreted, that he may enter into the feeling and atmosphere of it.

(a) Take time to study your instrument and to learn its resources thoroughly; do not follow any stereotyped registration absolutely, or any conventional directions, but make your own experiments. The lazy way is, of course, the easy way, but it seldom produces unusually interesting results in color. Be sure you know all the possibilities of your instrument. The registration indicated by composers on their published works is necessarily either quite general, or suited to some one particular organ, but it is suggestive of the effects desired. If you happen to have just the same

52

organ, or if the requirements are very simple, it may apply perfectly, but you should always try it out to make sure it will yield the desired effect. Some other registration may be much more suitable on your particular organ than that indicated on the music. Always work out for every composition, therefore, the registration best suited to your organ (or to the organ on which you are going to play it at any time) and write that registration down on your music in order to make sure of retaining it, and to save time at the performance.

SETTING UP THE PISTONS OF THE ORGAN

As an organist frequently finds it necessary to play a strange organ without having much time to get acquainted with it, it is advisable to use a definite system of setting up the adjustable pistons, so that certain solo stops, certain groups of stops — that is to say certain colors — shall be always identified with certain pistons; thus no organ will be entirely strange.

For instance: let Piston 1 on Great, Choir, and Swell represent the softest stop; Piston 2, pure String tone; Piston 3, pure Flute tone; Piston 4, Diapason tone. Reserve certain pistons for distinctive and variable combinations, as, for instance, the last one on the Swell for the orchestral combination described later in this chapter. Associate solo stops with certain pistons, as, for example, the Clarinet with the last piston in the Choir; put the solo stop you are going to use most frequently where it will be easiest to find. Only the barest suggestions can be offered here; a concert organist will have definite associations with every one of probably fifty pistons; work out a more elaborate scheme to meet your needs. It does not so much matter what your system is as that you have one according to which you can set up an organ quickly and in a manner familiar to you, and so avoid great waste of time and nervous energy by rendering all strange organs more or less familiar.

REGISTRATION OF PRE-BACH MUSIC

The question of registration of pre-Bach music is one which sooner or later presents itself to the student. The playing of this early music with simple stops, employing only the resources of the archaic organ, is appropriate and interesting in its quaintness for an occasional number, but it is not advisable to give whole recitals or very long sections of recitals in this manner, continuously, as, if it is insisted upon for too long a stretch, the audience wearies of something so remote from its time and temper. The argument for the invariable use of archaic registration is the same as for giving Shakespeare's plays without scenery, which is undoubtedly an interesting variation, permits attention to concentrate on their structure and lines, and is therefore, sometimes, most illuminating; nevertheless, it is hardly to be advocated as an unvarying rule of presentation. After all, the pre-Bach composers and Shakespeare alike did as they did because they "could no other"; of a certainty they employed all the resources they could command. Indeed they continually devised new ones, which would seem to argue that they would not by any means ignore what the modern organ — or the modern stage — can offer as aids in the interpretation of their thoughts and emotions.

COLOR THROUGH STOP COMBINATIONS

To illustrate the effect of combination on the color of a stop, and as a suggestion of the way to proceed to study stop combinations and blending the following examples may serve:

(a) To color a Diapason:

If you want clear Diapason quality, use it alone; if you desire a fuller, rounder tone, add a brilliant 8-foot Flute; if you want to intensify the serious, "churchly" effect, use with the Diapason a 16-foot Bourdon (Gedackt); to brighten the tone, add a 4-foot Flute; to imitate the ancient full-organ tone — when playing old Church music, for instance — use 16-foot, 8-foot, 4-foot, and 2-foot Flutes with the Diapason.

The Flute is the great color medium which is added to other stops or families of stops to shade their tones or to produce new tones; this because it is the lowest in the color scale, the most neutral and least assertive in character.

(b) To color a Flute:

Any coloring of a Flute amounts to intensifying its own color. Add a 16-foot Flute, and the color becomes serious or somber; to brighten the tone, add a 4-foot; to make it still lighter, a 2-foot. A piquant effect, suitable, for example, to a "pastoral" movement, is obtained by adding a Quintadena, which is a Flute that sounds also the second overtone — the Fifth — slightly. A similar effect is obtained by adding a Nazard, which sounds the Twelfth.

(c) To color a String:

String tone in combination with Flute tone of the same pitch, as an 8-foot String with an 8-foot Flute, gives a quality like that of a stringy Diapason; strangely enough, the use of this combination is considerably overdone, although it produces an uninteresting, monotonous tone.

A 4-foot Flute added to an 8-foot String will sometimes produce a tone of silvery quality, of character sufficiently distinctive for use in solo passages.

A 16-foot Bourdon with an 8-foot String in the low range gives a somber tone quality, appropriate for solemn or mysterious music, or, for example, for Funeral Marches. Even in the very low range the String brings out the pitch while the Flute adds somber quality, whereas, if in this low range the Bourdon were combined with an 8-foot Diapason or an 8-foot Flute the result would be indefinite and muddy.

It is advisable to use the powerful Strings with attention and care, as they do not always blend with the Diapasons; they are apt to retain their own tone quality too strongly and to stand out as a distinct entity. The more stringy the tone of the Diapasons the better the blending.

(d) To color a Reed, as, for example, an Oboe:

If you desire characteristic Oboe quality, use it alone; if you wish to "sing" a melody with violin tone quality, add an 8-foot Flute; to make the tone cheerful and gay, use a 4-foot Flute with the Oboe; to imbue it with serious, meditative character, use a 16-foot Flute with it; if you wish it to take on a piquant effect, which is occasionally desirable in a *Scherzo*, use with it a 2-foot Flute, a Piccolo.

A Diapason added to a Reed gives more "body," roundness, or sonorousness of tone; added to the Oboe, the resulting tone approaches the quality of a Cornopean.

COLOR THROUGH THE USE OF COUPLERS

Through the use of Couplers the color of a stop may also be changed as, for example, a combination of a 4-foot Flute on the Great and a Clarinet on the Choir, with the Choir to Great 16-foot Coupler drawn, produces a distinctive and interesting color unobtainable by any other means.

ORCHESTRAL EFFECT

All Strings there are on the Swell, together with the Vox Humana and Tremulant, with the couplers Swell to Swell 16-foot and 4-foot drawn, will most nearly approach the tone of the body of Strings in an orchestra. When you are playing in the upper register the addition of a 16-foot Bourdon will enhance this effect; if you happen to have a very cutting, "stringy" Reed it may also be added.

COLOR IN THE SOLO WITH ACCOMPANIMENT

3. (a) A third study in color is the solo with accompaniment. This is the easiest coloring for the organist to achieve, as, for instance, by means of the use of a soft String or Flute on the Choir for the accompaniment, an Oboe on the Swell for the solo, with, possibly, a 4-foot Flute on the Great for a counter melody. Because the effect in compositions of this character is gained with relatively slight effort the organist must beware of too frequent yielding to their easy delights, with resultant neglect of music which it demands more skill to make interesting.

(b) Another form of soloing, and one which makes greater demands, is Trio playing, or developing two melodies and a bass simultaneously. This offers an opportunity to contrast the small solo stops of an organ delightfully. Even on a very small organ the employment of simple Flute, String, and Diapason will afford considerable variety of color.

COLOR IN MODERN MUSIC

4. An interesting study in color is presented in modern music in the weaving in and out, as it were, of various color lines simultaneously, against a background.

Modern music is, on the whole, more colorful than ancient, because it is written in the expectation of being able to obtain color effects, and therefore provides opportunities for them, through contrasting passages and smaller phrases. It is made in blocks, as it were, instead of in large outlines; its phrases are not long, distinct lines as in the Trio, but short interweavings of several voices in and out of a background. From this background they become occasionally sharply detached, but are sometimes barely discernible within it when a slight change of color makes them perceptible. In such music changes of color may be frequent, therefore, without interfering with its outline; what would be violent and excessive color if applied to the older music may be perfectly natural, even indispensable in the interpretation of many modern compositions.

Nevertheless, even the most modern composition must be studied in its outlines and *colored within them*, in such fashion as not to interrupt them or to break the flow and curve of them, but to enrich and beautify them. Too frequent change of color may destroy entirely the line of a piece, rendering it choppy, depriving it of all continuity, and thus defeating its intention and spoiling its effect just as thoroughly as would a deadly monotony in its rendering.

CELESTA AND CHIMES AS AIDS TO COLOR

Two percussion stops which appear on large organs for the sole purpose of creating atmosphere are the Celesta and the Chimes. If they are to fulfil their purpose they must not be used too frequently, or inappropriately.

The Celesta may be used not only for harp-like effects, but, in combination with other soft stops, as the Dulciana, Erzähler, Spitz Flute, to lend a certain "ping" to the tone, which is felt as a change of color without the stop being recognizable.

THE DEVELOPMENT OF A SENSE OF COLOR

One of the greatest aids in the development of your sense of color is to *use it* in the sort of experimentation here indicated, and also in listening to music. Make an effort to hear great artists on any instrument whenever possible, and all the orchestral music you can. Much can be gained also by some study of and careful attention to the kindred arts, especially the arts of architecture and painting. From the former you can learn much concerning line, decoration, and climax; from the latter, color-blending and dramatic effects of color, light, and shade. Yet their chief value does not lie in what they may definitely teach you, but in the enrichment of your comprehension of the world of feeling, and of your sense of proportion, of color, and of beauty, and in the realization of the value of worthy, exalted, or exquisite expression of these things.

PART II
MUSIC

Section I
MANUALS ALONE

Attack and Release

LEGATO PLAYING: SUBSTITUTION
Each of the following exercises is to be played in all keys. Maintain a perfect legato in playing.

Substitution on Single Notes

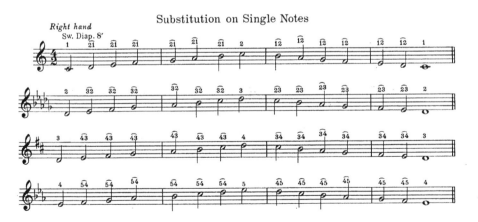

2

Substitution in Thirds

Substitution in Sixths

Each hand separately, then both hands together.

Substitution in Chords

Each hand separately, then both hands together.

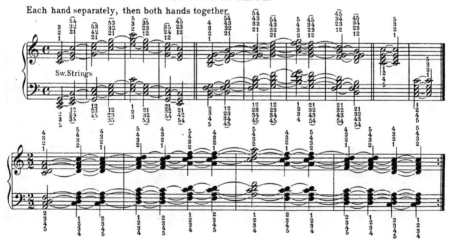

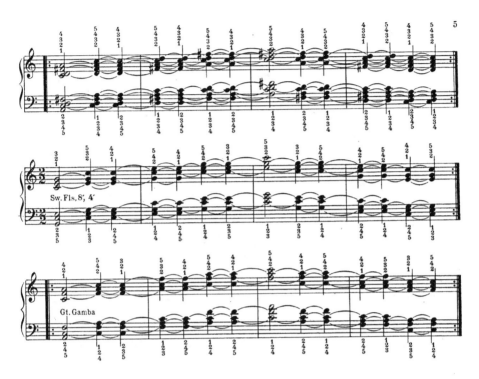

Substitution in Moving Parts

Substitution in Several Parts

The Student should finger the following pieces

Chorale Prelude

Exception: Thirds so rapidly played that Substitution is impossible

12

Hand Substitution

Substitution of one hand for the other on single notes played legato, with separated chords.

Sw. Bd. 16; Strings 8; Fl. 4'

Andante con moto

Substitution of one hand for the other in Chords

14

Substitution of one hand for the other in sustained chords in involved passages

Ch. Fl. 8′

Adagio

SECTION II
Pedal Alone.   Alternate Feet

Up and Down Movement of the Ankle

Play first with left toe, then with right toe

Pedal Bourdon 16', Sw. to Ped. = Swell Diapason and Flute 4'

Repeat the above exercises on other keys

Side to Side Movement of the Ankle

Right foot
non legato

Left foot non legato

The sign ∧ placed above a note indicates that it is to be played with the toe of the right foot
The sign ∧ placed below a note indicates that it is to be played with the toe of the left foot
The sign ∪ placed above a note indicates that it is to be played with the heel of the right foot
The sign ∪ placed below a note indicates that it is to be played with the heel of the left foot

Legato
a) b) c) d) e)

Repeat the above exercise, beginning on each black and white key from 𝄢 to 𝄢

Right foot moving, left foot repeating one note

Left foot moving, right foot repeating one note

On the Black Keys: Right foot moving, left foot repeating one note

Thirds

Various Intervals in Different Rhythms

SECTION III

Manuals and Pedal in Combination

Pedal part for Alternate feet only

Adjacent Notes in the Pedal Part

Left hand; various intervals in the pedal

22

Both hands; various intervals in the pedal

simile

Allegretto
Sw. Fls. 8', 4'
Ped. Bd. 16' Sw. to Ped.

Sw.

Thirds in the Pedal Part

Fourths in the Pedal Part

Fifths in the Pedal Part

Sixths in the Pedal Part

Sevenths in the Pedal Part

Octaves in the Pedal Part

Diapasons 8′, 16′, Pedal 16′, 8′, Gt. to Pedal

Allegro

Allegro

29

Adagio

Trio

SCHNEIDER

Ch. Clar., Ch. to Ch. 16′

Sw. Fls. 8′, 4′

Ped. Bd. 16′, Camba 16′, Ged. 8′

sempre staccato

30

SECTION IV
Pedal Alone
Heel and Toe

Sw. Flutes 8', 4'
Ped. Bd. 16', 8'; Sw. to Ped.

34

36

On the initials of Bach's name: B-A-C-H

Sequential passage in both music and pedalling.

SECTION V
Manuals Alone

LEGATO PLAYING

(a) Thumb and finger glissando.   (b) Crossing the longer fingers over the shorter.

Thumb Glissando

Maintain a perfect legato throughout the following exercises.
Each hand separately, then both together, in all keys.

Both hands

Chromatic Scale, legato;   Thumb glissando

Finger Glissando

40

Chords Glissando

Varied Applications of Glissando

ABT VOGLER

The student should mark the fingering, registration and expression in the following number.

Con moto

44

Crossing the longer fingers over the shorter

The student should mark the fingering, registration and expression in the following two pieces.

SECTION VI
Manuals and Pedal in Combination

Pedal part for heel and toe

Gt. Diaps. 16; 8; 4'
Ped. Diaps. 16; 8; Gt. to Ped.

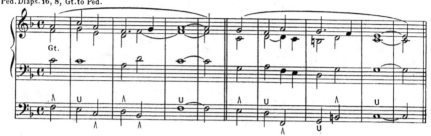

Sw. Flues 8; 4' Oboe, Sw. to Gt.
Gt. Diaps. 8; Fls. 8; 4'
Ped. Diap. II, Gt. and Sw. to Ped.

Con moto

Sw. Full, Sw. to Gt.
Gt. Flues 8; 4'
Ped. Flues 16; 8; Gt. and Sw. to Ped.

50

Moderato

Full Organ

Gt. Diaps. 16', 8', Oct. 4', Fifteenth 2'
Ped. Diaps. 16', 8', Gt. to Ped.

52

Sw. Full, Sw. to Sw. 4'
Ped. All Flues, Sw. to Ped. 8', 4'

Allegro marziale

Ch. Full
Ped. Diap. II, Bds. 16', 8', Ch. to Ped.

Moderato

Sw. Full, to Gt.
Gt. Flues16; 8; 4'
Ped. Full, to Gt. and Sw.

From Sonata I

Allegro assai vivace

MENDELSSOHN

legato

Postlude

M. HILARION ESLAVA
(1807-1878)

Cresc. Ped. on

Sw. Viole d'Orchestre, Celeste, Sw. to Ch.
Ch. Geigen Principal (Diap.)
Ped. Bd. 16; Sw. to Ped.

Elevation

ALEXANDRE GUILMANT

56

Sw. Vox Humana, Spitz Fl.,
    Vox Angelica, Sw. to Ch.
Ch. Ged. 16'
Ped Bd. 32', Gamba 16', Ged. 16', 8'

Adagio

CÉSAR FRANCK

58

Canzona

FRESCOBALDI
(1583 - 1644)

Chorale Prelude
On The Ancient Christmas Carol
"IN DULCI JUBILO"

Sw. Ob., Fl. 4; (Sw. to Sw. 16')
Gt. Clarabella, Fl. 4'
Ch. Dul. Geigen Principal
   (Ch. to Ch. 4')
Ped. Dul. 16; Ged 16; 8'
(For a two manual organ
Substitute Gt. for Ch. throughout)

J. S. BACH
(1685 - 1750)
Edited by
Clarence Dickinson

63

OSSIA

SECTION VII
Part-Playing
Harmonic and Polyphonic
Hymns and Chorales

Dividing the Inner Parts between the Hands

Chorale: "In Deep Distress on Thee I Call"

PAUL HOFHAIMER
(1459-1537)

Allegretto
sempre legato

ALCOCK

*) Reprinted from "The Organ" by W. G. Alcock, by permission of Novello and Company, Ltd.

65

Chorale Prelude
"Our Father in Heaven"

J. S. BACH

Sw. 16; 8; 4; Sw. to Gt.
Gt. Flues 8; 4'

Repeated Notes

When a note is repeated immediately in the same part play each note separately; when in a different part, tie them.   See Part I, Chapter IV.

68

Chorale
"All Men Must Die"

Gt. Foundation Stops 8; 4'

Sw. Soft 8; 4', Sw. to Gt.
Gt Soft 8'
Ped. Bd. 16; Gamba 16; Sw. and Gt. to Ped.

ALCOCK

*) Andante con moto

* Reprinted from "The Organ" by W. G. Alcock, by permission of Novello and Company, Ltd.

Sw. Full, Sw to Gt.
Gt Diaps. 8', Fls. 8', 4'
Ped Flues 16', 8', Sw. to Ped., Gt. to Ped.
Cresc. Ped. on

Prelude and Fugue

HANDEL

The phrasing should be marked by the student.

Con spirito

Fugue

The phrasing of all parts should be marked by the student according to the principles of Part-playing.

Allegro moderato

Chorale
"Blessed Jesu, We Are Here"

Sw. Strs., Sw. to Gt.
Gt. Soft 16', 8'
Ped. Bd. 32', 16', 8'

J. S. BACH

Hymn-Playing

"Rejoice Greatly O my Soul"

Harmonized by
J.S. BACH

a) Played on the manuals only

Sw.
Flues 8′, 4′

b) Played on manual and pedal

Gt.Diaps

16′ & 8′, Gt. coupled

c) Played on two different manuals and pedals; the melody treated as solo.

Part-Playing in Hymns.

W. H. MONK

Sun of my. Soul.

W. H. MONK

"Hursley" is written as follows:

Sun of my soul,— Thou Sa - viour dear, It is not night if Thou— be near; O may no earth - born cloud a - rise To hide Thee from— Thy ser - vant's eyes.

Played as follows:

SECTION VIII
Pedal Scales

a) Pedal Alone
b) Pedal with Manuals

Pedal Glissando

The Major Scales for Pedal

The student should fill out the exercise on each scale according to the plan of those preceding.

The Harmonic Minor Scales for Pedal

The Melodic Minor Scales for Pedal

Scales played with one foot

Scales running two Octaves

a) Major Scales running two Octaves

b) Minor Scales running two Octaves

84

Scale passages

The pedalling of the following should be marked by the student.

Sw: Diapasons
Ped: Violone, Bd. 16', 8',

Allegretto

86

Sw. Bd. 16', Strs, Sw. to Sw. 16', Sw. to Gt. 16', 8'
Gt.   Diap. II, Fl's, 8', 4'
Ped. Diap. II, Violone 16', Bd. 16', 8', Sw. to Ped.

Sw: Foundation Stops 8′, 4′
Gt : Diap. 8′, Sw. to Gt.
Pedal: **Bd.** 16′, 8′, Sw. to Ped.

Andante

Chromatic Scale

Sw.

Gt.

Gt.

Gt. to Ped.

rit.

88

Chorale
"Ah! What shall I, Poor Sinner, do?"

J. S. BACH

From Sonata IV
Pedal Scale

Allegro maestoso e vivace
Full Organ

MENDELSSOHN

SECTION IX
Manipulation of the Swell Pedal
Balancing Two Swell Pedals
FROM "REVERIE"

DICKINSON

Sw. Ob., Trem.
Ch. Unda Maris, Ch. to Ch. 4´
Ped. Ged. 16´, 8´

St. Cecilia Series No 79   Copyright, 1917, by The H. W. Gray Co.

Adagio

MENDELSSOHN

Sw. Cornopean
Ch. Flutes 8´, 4´
Ped. Bd. 16´, Violone 16´;
Sustained melody in left hand, legato thirds and sixths in right hand, and staccato pedal.

SECTION X
Touches Other than Legato
(a) SEMI-DETACHED (b) MARCATO

Semi-detached Touch
Sw. Strs. 8', Flutes 8'; 4'; Sw. to Gt.
Gt. Flute 8

ORA PRO NOBIS

Sw. Bd 16', Unda Maris, Solo Mix.Trem.
Ch. Concert Fl 8'
Ped. Dul 16'

The melody was brought to Liszt from Jerusalem.

FRANZ LISZT
Edited by
Clarence Dickinson

Copyright, 1921, by The H. W. Gray & Co.

93

Marcato Touch
Sw. Full, to Gt.
Gt. *mf*
Ped. *f* Sw. and Gt. to Ped.

*)Postlude

W. T. BEST

Allegro spiritoso

*) By kind permission of Novello & Co.,Ltd.

Processional March

Sw. Full
Gt. Full
Ped. Full, Gt. and Sw. to Ped.

ALEXANDRE GUILMANT

100

D.C. senza replica

SECTION XI
Touches other than Legato
Staccato

(a) Single Notes (b) Chords

Prélude

Sw. Ob.
Gt. Clarabella or Wald Fl., Viole d'Amour
Ch. Fl. 8; Pic. 2' or Fl. 4' Celesta 4'
Ped. Bd. 16; Dul 16; Ged. 8'

Edited by Clarence Dickinson

LOUIS NICOLAS CLÉRAMBAULT
(1676-1749)

Arranged by Alexandre Guilmant

Copyright, 1921, by The H. W. Gray Co.

Chorale
From Sonata VI

Staccato Pedal
Gt. Diaps, 16; 8'
Ped. Diaps., Strs., 16; 8'

MENDELSSOHN

Sw: Orchestral Oboe
Gt: Clarabella 8′
Ch: Concert Fl., Fl. Cel., Ch. to Gt.
Ped: Bourdon 16′, Gamba 16′, Bd .8′

Edited by Clarence Dickinson

Sœur Monique

(Sister Monica)

FRANÇOIS COUPERIN
(1668-1733)
Arranged by Alexandre Guilmant

Expressively, but without dragging

Solo: Reeds, Solo to Gt.
Sw. : Full, Sw. to Gt.
Gt. : Diap.
Ped.: Flues 32', 16', 8', Solo, Sw. and Gt. to Ped.

From "Etude"

PAUL HELD

Staccato Chords
Sw. Diaps. 8′, Reeds 8′, 4′
Gt. Diaps. 8′, Reeds 8′, 4′
Ped. Diaps. 16′, 8′, Sw. and Gt. to Ped.

Fanfare

JACQUES LEMMENS

Allegro non troppo

114

SECTION XII
Pedal
(A) Crossing the Feet
(B) Substitution
(C) Skips of a Third

Crossing the feet

Substitution of a heel for a toe or vice versa.

118

Sw. Stings
Ch. Clarinet
Ped. Bd 16' Fl.8'

Adagio

From Sonata III

Sw. Strs.
Gt. Diap. II
Ch. Fls 8′ 4′
Ped. Bd. 16′, Sw. to Ped.

Mendelssohn

piano e dolce

Sw. Foundation Stops, Sw. to Gt.   Substitution on a repeated note
Gt. Diaps. 8′
Ped. Violone 16′, Bd. 16′, 8′; Gt. and Sw. to Ped.

Skips of a third

124

SECTION XIII

(a) Crossing the hands
(b) Trios

Crossing the hands

Sw. Orchestral Ob. or Flügel Horn
Gt. Gamba or Gamba Cel.
Ch. Fls · 8′, 4′,
Ped. Gamba 16, Ged. 16′, 8′

*) Trio

FREDERIC ARCHER

*) By kind permission of Norello & Co.,Ltd.

130

Crossing the hands
Sw. Voix Celeste
Ch. Quintadena, Fl. 4′
Ped. Ged. 16′, 8′,

Trio

RHEINBERGER

Andante

132
Sw. Ob., Fl. 4'
Gt. Fl. 8'
Ch. Clar.,
Ped.Ged. 16', 8', Gamba 16',8', Fag.16'

Christmas Pastorale
"From Heaven High To Earth I Come"

JOHANN PACHELBEL
(1653-1706)
Edited by Clarence Dickinson

Allegretto quasi Andantino

MANUAL

PEDAL

134

Trio

Sw: Oboe
Gt: Fl.8'
Ch: Clarinet
Ped: Ged.16,8; Gamba 16'

J. L. KREBS
(1713-1780)
Edited by Clarence Dickinson

SECTION XIV
Manual and Pedal Arpeggios

Ch. Fls. 8', 4', Celesta 4'

Andante con moto

From
Processional March

On Two Church Hymns
"Iste Confessor" and "Ecce Sacerdos Magnus"

Fantasia

Manual Arpeggios and Rolled Chords
Sw: Stop. Diap. Vox Humana, Gamba and Voix Céleste with Tremulant
Ch: Dulciana and Flute 8′
Gt: Bd. 16′ with Sw. coupled in Unison and lower octave (ad lib.)
Ped: Bd. 16′ Ch. to Ped.

ALEXANDRE GUILMANT

Pedal Arpeggios

Rapid Arpeggios

142

Seventh Chord Arpeggios, various keys

144

From Toccata in C Major

Ped.32; 16; 8' and 4' with Reeds

Allegro moderato

PEDAL SOLO

J.S.BACH

*) Prelude

STEGGALL

First time, Legato Pedal.
Second time, Staccato Pedal.

Maestoso

Full Organ

*) From Instruction Book for the Organ by Charles Steggall, by kind permission of Novello & Co., Ltd.

Postlude

C. AD. THOMAS

148

150

poco riten.

SECTION XV
Changing Manuals

Monochromatic
registration:
{
Sw.   Diap. I, Fl. 4´, Sw. to Gt. and Ch.
Gt.   Diap. II, Fl. 4´
Ch.   Diap., Fl. 4´, Ch to Gt.
}

Polychromatic
registration:
{
Sw.   Strs. 8´, Fl. 4´
Gt.   Fls. 8´, 4´
Ch.   Clar., Fl. 4´
}

J. S. BACH

Partita

Caprice

Sw: Bourdon 16', Flute 4'
Gt: Diap.II, Claribel Fl.
Ch: Clar., Pic. 2'
Ped: Bourdon 16', Gamba 16', Violone 16', Fl.Dolce 8'

ALEXANDRE GUILMANT
Edited by
Clarence Dickinson

164

SECTION XVI
Playing on Two Manuals
at the same time with one hand

Sw: Vox Humana (soft strings)
Gt: Fl. 4′
Ch: Dul., Flute d'Amour 4′, Celesta 4′
Ped: Ged.16′, 8′, Dulciana 16′

Prayer in F

ALEXANDRE GUILMANT
Edited by Clarence Dickinson

✤ On a two manual organ the accompaniment may be played on the Gt. an octave lower.

SECTION XVII

Fugues and Other Four-Part Playing

Fughetta

Sw. Full
Gt. *mf*
Ped. Diap. 16 Sw. and Gt. to Ped.

J. E. REMBT

Prelude and Fugue

Sw: Full, to Gt. & Ch.
Gt: Diaps. 8; Fls. 8; 4'
Ch: Full
Ped: Full except Reeds, Sw. and Gt. to Ped.
Cresc. Ped. on

J. S. BACH

Moderato

Gt.

172

Andante
From Sonata VI

Sw.Voix Cel.,Vox Angelica, Sw. to Gt. 8, 4'
Gt Dulciana
Ped. Ged. 16', Bd.16', Sw.to Ped.

MENDELSSOHN

Sw: Cornopean
Ch: Dulcet
Ped. Bd.16', Ged. 16', 8'
Gamba 16'

Chorale Prelude
"O Sacred Head Surrounded"

J.S.BACH
Edited by Clarence Dickinson

SECTION XVIII
Ornaments·

Solo Engl. Hr.
Sw. Ob.
Gt. Fl. 8'
Ch. Quint., Fl. 4'
Ped. Ged. 16; 8', Dul. 16'

Adagio
Sonata **IV**

J.S.BACH

* See also: "Soeur Monique", Couperin, p. 106, and "Trio", Krebs, p. 134

SECTION XIX
Pedal
a) Octaves, Sixths, Thirds, Chords
b) Double pedal with Manuals

Octaves
Care must be taken that both notes sound simultaneously.

The student should play all the scales in octaves, so far as possible.

182

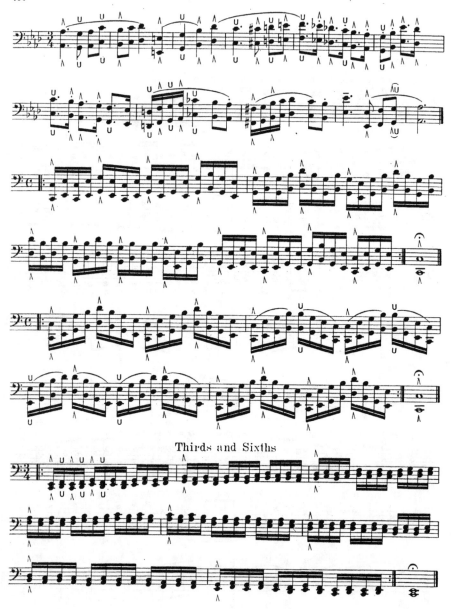

Thirds and Sixths

The student should play the other scales in Thirds.

The student should play the other scales in sixths.

184

Pedal Solos Involving Various Intervals

Allegro marziale

188

Marche Réligieuse

On the theme of the chorus "Lift up
Your Heads, O Ye Gates" from Handel's "The Messiah"

Sw. Flues and Reeds 8; 4; Sw. to Gt. and Ch.
Gt. 16; 8; 4; Foundation Stops
Ch. Full
Ped. Flues 16; 8; Sw. to Ped.

ALEXANDRE GUILMANT
Edited by
Clarence Dickinson

Allegro moderato e maestoso

MANUAL

PEDAL

St. Cecilia No 156

SECTION XX
Pedal

a) Extended Glissando
b) Two Etudes for Pedal Alone

Extended Pedal Glissando

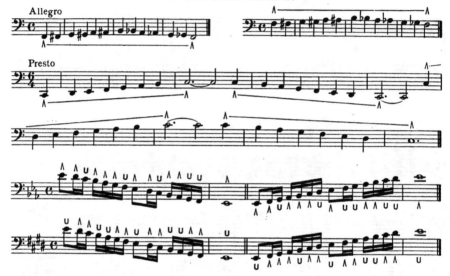

Etude
For Pedal Alone

Sw. Ob. Corn. Trem.
Gt. Diaps. 8', Fls. 8', Tuba 8', Trem.
Ped. Bd. 32', 16', Gamba 16', 8', Sw. to Ped.

ALKAN
Edited by Clarence Dickinson

200

Etude
For Pedal Alone

ALKAN
Edited by Clarence Dickinson

Sw. *mf* to Ped.
Ct. *mf* to Ped.
Ped. *mf*

202

The *First* and *Only* Book Published on

THE ART OF TRANSCRIBING FOR THE ORGAN

A complete Text Book
for the Organist

in arranging

Choral and Instrumental Music

By

HERBERT F. ELLINGFORD

Mus. Bac. Oxon.

Organist to the City of Liverpool at

ST. GEORGE'S HALL

The first and only book published on this important topic by a practical master of the subject. Every organist is nowadays compelled to transcribe all sorts of compositions for his instrument for church or concert use. This book gives him the actual technique which enables him to do so. For the choral and orchestral works there is given a full page score, its pianoforte equivalent, and the method by which it is transferred to the organ. The scheme includes, small orchestra, string orchestra, chamber and pianoforte music and songs. With this book the whole world of music becomes available at the organ bench.

There are 216 musical illustrations in the book, of which 137 are transcriptions, and 79 full-scores by such composers as Haydn, Mozart, Beethoven, Mendelssohn, Brahms, Schubert, Schumann, Weber, Wagner, Tschaikowsky, Grieg, Smetana. Chopin, Sullivan, and Rachmaninoff.

SUBSCRIPTION PRICE $4.00

NEW YORK ∴ THE H. W. GRAY CO.

SOLE AGENTS FOR NOVELLO & CO., Ltd., LONDON

CPSIA information can be obtained
at www.ICGtesting.com
Printed in the USA
BVHW04s0338130418
513210BV00002B/156/P